T0274772

EMPOWER YOUR NONPROFIT

AMY NEUMANN

EMPOWER YOUR NONPROFIT

SIMPLE WAYS TO CO-CREATE WITH
AI FOR PROFOUND IMPACT

WILEY

Published by John Wiley & Sons, Inc., Hoboken, New Jersey.
Published simultaneously in Canada.

For general information on our other products and services or for technical support, please contact our Customer Care Department within the United States at (800) 762-2974, outside the United States at (317) 572-3993 or fax (317) 572-4002.

Wiley also publishes its books in a variety of electronic formats. Some content that appears in print may not be available in electronic formats. For more information about Wiley products, visit our web site at www.wiley.com.

Library of Congress Cataloging-in-Publication Data is Available:

ISBN: 9781394263240 (cloth)
ISBN: 9781394263257 (ePub)
ISBN: 9781394263264 (ePDF)

Cover Design: Wiley
Cover Image: © devastudios/Adobe Stock
Author Photo: Courtesy of Amy Neumann
SKY10085532_091924

For Isabella Skye and other curious minds

Contents

Introduction

There is nothing more exciting than being inspired by a vision for making a difference in the world and imagining a way to actually change it for good. But nothing is more daunting than being in a nonprofit organization with that vision and not having all the tools and systems to allow you to achieve that dream.

This book aims to empower nonprofits with simple ways to co-create with artificial intelligence (AI) to make a profound impact. There is a wealth of research, resources, and information about AI advancements, tools, and systems that can facilitate the actual achievement of tangible goals. You will learn how AI can assist in achieving those dreams to change the world better than any technology before AI.

The Hummingbird Effect: How AI Can Empower Your Nonprofits

Imagine a hummingbird, a tiny burst of emerald feathers. Despite its size, it can hover, dart, and dive at lightning speed. It sips nectar from the most delicate blooms, seemingly defying gravity with its energy. Through its hurried visits, this tiny yet ambitious creature plays a vital role in pollinating plants, ensuring the continuation of life in the ecosystem.

In the same way, AI can be a powerful tool for nonprofits. Though unseen, it can act with incredible speed and agility, flitting through vast amounts of data to identify patterns, predict trends, and optimize actions. Just as the hummingbird's dazzling energy contributes to a thriving ecosystem, AI can empower nonprofits to achieve their missions with greater efficiency and impact.

Here's how the hummingbird analogy connects to AI's benefiting a nonprofit organization:

Tiny but Mighty:
AI, like the hummingbird, can be surprisingly powerful despite its seeming simplicity.

Agile and Adaptable:
AI can quickly analyze data and adjust strategies, mimicking the hummingbird's ability to change direction

Source: Image created by AI Art Generator DALL-E-3

instantly. Hummingbirds are incredibly fast and agile, able to change direction as needed. Similarly, nonprofits can use AI to be nimble and responsive, quickly pivoting strategies based on real-time data and insights to serve their mission better. In many cultures, hummingbirds symbolize resilience, endurance, and adaptability. By integrating AI, nonprofits demonstrate their commitment to continuously learning, evolving, and finding innovative ways to deliver on their mission in the face of challenges.

Reaches the Inaccessible:

AI can explore complex datasets, reaching insights that might be hidden to the human eye, like the hummingbird accessing nectar deep within flowers.

Performs Unique and Unimaginable Tasks:

Hummingbirds are the only birds that can fly backward. With AI, nonprofits can look back at historical data to gain new insights while also forecasting forward to anticipate trends and proactively adapt.

Creates a Ripple Effect:

AI, like the hummingbird pollinating plants, can profoundly impact the organization's overall success by optimizing processes and identifying opportunities. Despite their small size, hummingbirds have a big impact as prolific pollinators. AI can help nonprofits "pollinate" their data, spreading insights and best practices to drive significant impact, even with limited resources.

Precision:

Hummingbirds are known for their precision and ability to target individual flowers. AI can help nonprofits precisely target their interventions, personalizing outreach and services for specific individuals or communities to drive more tailored and effective support.

Amplified Storytelling and Communications:

Hummingbirds are often seen as messengers of hope and joy. Nonprofits can leverage AI to amplify storytelling, spread inspiring messages of impact, and connect with supporters in powerful ways to spark hope and change.

Expanded Opportunities:

Just as hummingbirds are attracted to vibrant flowers, AI can help nonprofits uncover and be drawn to the most promising opportunities to drive colorful and meaningful change.

Like the hummingbird, this book is a testament to the power of seemingly small things to create a big impact. By co-creating with AI, your nonprofit can achieve its mission with greater efficiency and reach, leaving a lasting positive influence on the world. This book inspires you to realize that you can co-create with AI to facilitate your dreams and your nonprofit's mission.

Technological advancements have always reshaped industries and shifted how we live and work, and now AI has emerged as a powerful force for change. The nonprofit sector, driven by a mission to create positive social impact, is not immune to this technological paradigm shift. As organizations increasingly recognize the potential of AI to revolutionize their operations and amplify their impact, it is crucial to develop a deep understanding of these technologies and their implications for the future of the nonprofit sector.

Empower Your Nonprofit: Simple Ways to Co-create with AI for Profound Impact is a comprehensive guide designed to help nonprofit leaders navigate the complex landscape of AI and harness its power to drive their organizations forward. This book results from extensive research and interviews with various experts, including nonprofit executives, technology professionals, and AI researchers.

By bringing together these unique perspectives, this book aims to provide a balanced and practical understanding of AI in the nonprofit context. Through key interviews conducted both in writing and virtual video conversations, invaluable insights have been gained into the real-world applications of AI in nonprofits. From optimizing fundraising efforts and improving service delivery to enhancing impact measurement and driving operational efficiency, the examples and use cases presented in this book showcase the massive potential of AI across various aspects of nonprofit work.

However, this book is not just about the technical aspects of AI. It has resulted from years of experience and hundreds of hours of research in the nonprofit and AI spaces. Interviews with high-level executives in this space allowed for a real-time study of the strategic, operational, and ethical considerations nonprofits must navigate as they embark on their AI journey.

This book explores best practices, common challenges, and key lessons learned from organizations at the forefront of this technological shift. It is intended to equip nonprofit leaders with the knowledge and tools to make informed decisions about AI implementation. It will provide insights about how to "co-create" alongside AI, augmenting human skills while leveraging everything uniquely human to create more innovation.

Whether you are a nonprofit executive seeking to explore AI's potential for your organization, a technology professional looking to understand the unique challenges and opportunities of working with nonprofits, or simply someone passionate about the intersection of technology and social impact, this book has something to offer. By combining insights from nonprofit leaders and AI experts, we provide a comprehensive and accessible guide to AI in the social sector.

As you embark on this journey, it's important to approach AI not as a daunting challenge or a magical solution but as a powerful tool that can help nonprofits achieve their missions more effectively and efficiently when used responsibly and strategically. With the right knowledge, mindset, and approach, AI has the potential to revolutionize the way nonprofits operate and drive profound impact in the communities they serve.

CHAPTER 1

A Brief Overview of Artificial Intelligence

Artificial intelligence (AI) has emerged as one of the most potentially world-changing technological events to date. It can potentially revolutionize industries and reshape how we live and work.

As Devin Thorpe, CEO of The Super Crowd and author of *Superpowers for Good*, aptly puts it, "We have now arrived at the moment when avoiding the use of AI is like avoiding the use of the internet."

A Brief History of AI

Year	AI event/development	Impact perspective
1940s	Invention of electronic computers	The birth of modern computing, laying the foundation for future AI advancements.
1950	Claude Shannon's "Theseus" mouse	Early example of AI, where a mechanical mouse navigated a maze.
1956	Dartmouth Workshop	AI is officially born; the term "Artificial Intelligence" is coined.
1970s–1980s	Development of expert systems	Programs that mimicked the decision-making abilities of human experts, like early medical diagnosis systems.

(continued)

(continued)

Year	AI event/development	Impact perspective
1997	IBM's Deep Blue defeats chess champion Garry Kasparov	A computer beats a world chess champion, showcasing AI's strategic thinking capabilities.
2000s	Rise of machine learning and neural networks	AI starts to learn from data, leading to more accurate predictions and classifications.
2001	Release of the movie *A.I. Artificial Intelligence*	Hollywood brings AI to the big screen, increasing public interest and awareness.
2002	Introduction of Roomba, the autonomous vacuum cleaner	AI enters homes in the form of a smart cleaning device.
2011	IBM Watson wins *Jeopardy!*	AI demonstrates understanding and processing of natural language on a popular quiz show.
2011	Launch of Apple's Siri	AI-powered virtual assistants become mainstream with the introduction of Siri on iPhones.
2014	Amazon introduces Alexa	AI-powered voice assistant becomes a household name, controlling smart home devices and answering questions.
2014	Google's DeepMind beats professional Go players	AI shows advanced strategic thinking in the complex game of Go.
2016	Release of Pokémon Go, utilizing AR (augmented reality)	AI and AR merge in a popular mobile game, blending the real world with virtual creatures.
2017	Google develops the Transformer architecture	Behind-the-scenes breakthrough in AI that leads to improved language understanding and generation.
2018	Introduction of deepfake technology	AI creates realistic but fake videos, raising awareness about digital manipulation.
2018	Google's AI-powered Duplex makes a restaurant reservation over the phone	AI achieves a major milestone in natural-sounding conversational abilities.
2019	TikTok's AI-driven recommendation system takes the world by storm	AI curates personalized video feeds, driving the app's explosive popularity.

Year	AI event/development	Impact perspective
2020	AI aids in COVID-19 vaccine development	AI accelerates the research and development of vaccines, showcasing its potential in healthcare.
2021	Release of AI-generated music and artwork	AI starts to create original music and art, blurring the lines between human and machine creativity.
2021	Google announces LaMDA, a conversational AI	AI demonstrates more natural and engaging conversational abilities.
2022	Launch of ChatGPT	AI chatbot captivates the public with its ability to generate coherent and contextually relevant text.
2023	AI-integrated products like self-driving cars and smart home devices become more common	AI is seamlessly integrated into everyday life, making technology more intuitive and user-friendly.

Understanding AI and Harnessing the Power

Understanding and harnessing AI's power is no longer optional for nonprofit organizations; it is essential for driving innovation, efficiency, and impact in an increasingly complex and competitive landscape.

At its core, AI refers to developing computer systems that can perform tasks requiring human intelligence, such as visual perception, speech recognition, decision-making, and language translation. These systems are trained on vast amounts of data to recognize patterns, learn from experience, and make predictions or decisions without being explicitly programmed for every possible scenario.

AI encompasses various subfields and approaches, each with its techniques and applications. Machine learning, for example, enables systems to learn and improve their performance on a specific task over time without being explicitly programmed. Deep learning, a subset of machine learning based on artificial neural networks, allows AI to learn from unstructured data like text, images, and audio, opening new possibilities for analysis and insights.

Natural language processing (NLP) is another key area of AI that enables machines to understand, interpret, and generate human language. This technology powers applications like chatbots, sentiment analysis, and language translation, which can help nonprofits improve communication, engagement, and service delivery. Computer vision, meanwhile, allows AI to identify and process images and videos in ways that mimic human perception, with applications ranging from object recognition to facial analysis.

The potential applications of AI in the nonprofit sector are vast and varied. From optimizing fundraising efforts and improving donor engagement to streamlining operations and enhancing program delivery, AI can help nonprofits work smarter, faster, and more effectively. By automating routine tasks, analyzing complex datasets, and generating new insights, AI can free up human resources to focus on higher-level strategic priorities and mission-critical activities.

However, as with any powerful technology, AI presents challenges and risks that nonprofits must navigate carefully. Ensuring the ethical and responsible development and deployment of AI systems is critical, particularly when working with sensitive data or vulnerable populations. Issues like algorithmic bias, data privacy, and transparency must be addressed proactively to maintain trust and accountability.

Moreover, successful AI adoption requires more than just technical implementation; it also demands a cultural shift within organizations and new skills and mindsets among staff and stakeholders. Nonprofits must be willing to experiment, learn, and adapt as they integrate AI into their operations while focusing on their core missions and values.

Despite these challenges, the potential benefits of AI for nonprofits are too significant to ignore. As AI technology advances and becomes more accessible, organizations that embrace AI strategically and responsibly will be better positioned to drive impact, scale their efforts, and achieve their missions. The future of the nonprofit sector will be shaped by those who can effectively harness the power of AI to augment and enhance human capabilities while always keeping the well-being of the communities they serve at the forefront.

Importance of AI in the Nonprofit Sector

"Generative AI has the potential to change the world in ways that we can't even imagine. It has the power to create new ideas, products, and services that will make our lives easier, more productive, and more creative. It also has the potential to solve some of the world's biggest problems, such as climate change, poverty, and disease."[1]
    – Bill Gates, Microsoft Co-founder and Co-chair of the
Bill & Melinda Gates Foundation

The nonprofit sector is vital in addressing various social, environmental, and economic challenges. However, nonprofits often face resource constraints and increasing demands for their services. AI can revolutionize how nonprofits operate, enabling them to optimize their resources, enhance decision-making processes, and amplify their impact.

AI can help nonprofits increase efficiency and reduce costs by automating routine tasks, analyzing vast amounts of data, and personalizing communication with stakeholders. These capabilities allow organizations to focus their limited resources on mission-critical activities. AI can also improve fundraising efforts and donor engagement by analyzing donor data to predict giving patterns and optimize fundraising strategies. Additionally, AI-powered tools can help nonprofits personalize services and support for beneficiaries, ensuring that individuals receive the most relevant and impactful assistance.

Measuring and demonstrating impact is a crucial aspect of nonprofit work, and AI can play a significant role in this area. By analyzing data from various sources, AI can help organizations better understand their programs' effectiveness and identify areas for improvement. Furthermore, AI can assist nonprofits in identifying new opportunities for innovation and collaboration, fostering partnerships that can lead to greater impact.

As Julie A. Maurer, PhD, lead research manager at the Ohio Education Research Center at The Ohio State University, emphasizes:

> The nonprofit sector is evolving quickly, and choosing not to adopt AI solutions will increasingly disadvantage your organization in ways that may not be immediately obvious. The benefits of adopting new technologies are far-reaching and span your entire organization – from strategic planning to customer service, fundraising, and all other areas of the operation.

Maurer also highlights the importance of taking advantage of resources available to offset the costs involved, such as J.P. Morgan's Force for Good program, TechSoup's nonprofit marketplace, and Resourceful Nonprofit (the author's nonprofit).

It is important to note that while AI offers numerous benefits, its adoption requires careful planning, strategy, governance, and continuous human oversight. Nonprofits must proactively address concerns around ethical AI development, data privacy, and potential misuse. When implemented responsibly, AI provides an incredible opportunity for social impact organizations to extend their reach and augment their workforce while catalyzing their ability to understand and solve complex challenges.

It is becoming increasingly vital for nonprofit leaders to understand and leverage AI to stay competitive, adapt to changing circumstances, and maximize community impact.

RESPONSIBLE AND ETHICAL USE OF AI

Ensuring responsible and ethical use of AI is critical for nonprofits as they integrate these technologies into their operations. The following are several strategies nonprofits can employ and learn more about throughout this book.

Develop an AI Ethics Framework: Create ethical principles and guidelines that align with the nonprofit's mission and involve diverse stakeholders in their development.

Prioritize Transparency and Explainability: Ensure AI systems are transparent, provide clear explanations, and use interpretable models while being open with beneficiaries about AI use.

Address Bias and Fairness: Regularly assess for biases, use diverse datasets, and implement fairness audits to ensure equitable treatment by AI systems.

Ensure Data Privacy and Security: Implement strong data governance, adhere to data protection regulations, and use secure protocols to protect sensitive data.

Foster Human Oversight and Accountability: Ensure human oversight in AI decisions, establish clear responsibilities, and provide staff training for effective AI management.

Engage in Ongoing Monitoring and Evaluation: Continuously monitor AI systems, conduct regular audits, and be ready to adjust or decommission systems if they cause harm or fail ethical standards.

Foster Collaboration and Knowledge Sharing: Collaborate with other nonprofits and experts, participate in industry initiatives, and contribute to AI ethics discourse to enhance decision-making and share best practices.

ENHANCED DECISION-MAKING

AI can enhance decision-making in the nonprofit sector in several ways:

Predictive Analytics for Resource Allocation: AI algorithms can analyze historical data on program outcomes, beneficiary demographics, and funding sources to predict which initiatives will likely have the greatest impact. This information can help nonprofit leaders make data-driven decisions about where to allocate limited resources for maximum effect.

Sentiment Analysis for Strategic Planning: NLP techniques can analyze social media posts, news articles, and other public data sources to gauge public opinion on issues relevant to a nonprofit's mission. These insights can inform strategic planning decisions, such as which programs to prioritize or how to frame messaging for maximum resonance with target audiences.

Machine Learning for Grant Proposal Evaluation: AI can be trained on historical data about successful grant proposals to identify patterns and characteristics associated with funding success. This knowledge can then be applied to evaluate and optimize new grant proposals, increasing the likelihood of securing funding.

Predictive Maintenance for Facilities Management: AI can analyze sensor data and maintenance records for nonprofits that own or operate physical facilities to predict when equipment is likely to fail. This enables proactive maintenance that minimizes downtime and reduces repair costs, helping nonprofit leaders make more informed decisions about facilities management and budgeting.

Intelligent Dashboards for Performance Monitoring: AI-powered dashboards can integrate and analyze data from multiple sources (such as program metrics, financial data, and stakeholder feedback) to provide nonprofit leaders with real-time, holistic views of organizational performance. These insights can support data-driven decision-making and help leaders identify areas for improvement or course correction.

Simulation Modeling for Scenario Planning: AI can create detailed simulation models of complex social systems, allowing nonprofit leaders to test the potential impacts of different intervention strategies or policy changes before implementing them. This "what-if" scenario planning can lead to more robust and effective decision-making.

Computer Vision for Needs Assessment: AI algorithms can analyze satellite imagery or drone footage to assess infrastructure damage after a disaster, identify areas of need in underserved communities, or track changes in land use patterns over time. These insights can help nonprofit leaders make more informed decisions about where and how to deploy resources for maximum impact.

By prioritizing these strategies, nonprofits can help ensure that their use of AI is aligned with their missions and values and that these powerful technologies are being used to benefit society. As the use of AI in the nonprofit sector continues to grow, organizations must remain vigilant and proactive in addressing the ethical implications of these technologies.

Keeping Perspective

As you consider the integration of AI and its potential applications in the nonprofit sector, it is essential to consider and remember a few key perspectives that will help guide your journey and decision-making process.

THE CURRENT STAGE OF AI DEVELOPMENT

While AI has made remarkable strides in recent years, it is crucial to understand that, from an end-user perspective, the technology is still in its early stages. As with any nascent technology, AI is not infallible and may be subject to errors or misinformation. It is essential to approach AI critically and verify the accuracy of the outputs it generates. Maintain a healthy level of caution and skepticism, check facts, and always rely on human judgment to make final decisions.

Use a pragmatic approach to adapting the AI tools and systems essential to your needs. It is not usually necessary to get bogged down in trying to understand all the nuances of every aspect of the best AI tools available because AI development is an ever-evolving scenario.

THE IMPORTANCE OF ASKING GREAT QUESTIONS (CORRECT PROMPTING)

The quality of the results you obtain from AI systems heavily depends on the quality of the input you provide. This is particularly true for generative AI (Gen AI) models (Gen AI bots), which rely on user prompts to guide their output. Learning how to prompt AI systems effectively is a skill that requires practice and experimentation. As you work with AI tools, take the time to refine your prompts and learn how to elicit the most accurate and relevant responses. Effective prompting is a critical component of successful AI implementation, and experimenting with what works for specific projects and needs is helpful as you learn.

Honing skills in this area is critical to getting the desired output because of the importance of asking the right questions and providing the right data to generative AI chatbots (referred to in this book as Gen AI bots or chatbots).

A few considerations to think about are:

- Determine your desired output (a report, one-pager, presentation outline, grant draft, etc.).
- Provide the Gen AI chatbot with important contextual information, including attaching resources and documents (while not publicly sharing proprietary or personal data about your organization, donors, etc.).
- Provide further background, like who the audience for the output is (funders, beneficiaries, donors, volunteers, etc.), what type of voice you want to use (professional, casual, etc.), length, format, or other relevant initial items.
- If the task you request is very long, detailed, or complex, it may be wise to run your prompts in a sequence, one at a time, waiting for confirmation of understanding or output from the Gen AI bot after each step before requesting the next step.
- Often, many revisions of prompts – or using multiple Gen AI chatbots with different task strengths – can be helpful.

Many resources to learn prompt engineering exist from large tech companies, online course providers, and industry experts. And you can even ask various Gen AI bots to help you craft the perfect prompt for other bots (or themselves) to create exactly the output (achieve the goal) you want.

This can be particularly helpful when crafting visual elements, as the visual Gen AI image creation bots (DALL-E, Stable Diffusion, Midjourney, and similar) may respond best to prompts containing specific verbiage from the creative arts.

REAL-TIME RESEARCH APPROACH IN THIS BOOK

The insights and recommendations presented in this book result from years of work, research, and learning in the technical and AI space. Despite the growing interest in AI, it was clear that nonprofit-specific AI usage case studies and real-world examples are currently scarce. To bridge this gap, interviews were conducted with key thought leaders in the AI industry, business sector, and nonprofit space. These interviews provide valuable, real-time feedback, insights, and experiences that help paint a more comprehensive picture of how AI can be effectively leveraged in the nonprofit context.

THE IMPORTANCE OF DUE DILIGENCE – RESEARCH, PLANNING, AND EXPERIMENTATION

Before investing significant time and resources into AI implementation, conducting thorough research, planning, and experimentation is critical. Every nonprofit is unique, with its own set of challenges, goals, and resources. What works for one organization may not be the best fit for another. Take the time to explore the AI landscape, identify the tools and solutions that align with your organization's needs, and conduct small-scale pilots to test their effectiveness.

This iterative approach will help you make informed decisions and minimize the risk of costly missteps. Be sure to review the sections in this book concerning getting started in AI and the critical issues to address, such as data security, privacy, and bias in AI, and how to best approach deliberate implementation planning to meet your organization's specific needs.

MAINTAINING FOCUS ON YOUR MISSION AND IMPACT

As you explore the potential of AI for your nonprofit, it is essential always to keep your organization's mission at the forefront. AI is not a magic solution or a replacement for human expertise and judgment. Instead, it is a powerful tool that can help you amplify your impact and achieve your goals more effectively. Approach AI as a means of "co-creating" with technology – leveraging its capabilities to complement and enhance the skills and knowledge of your team to achieve your core purpose.

Remember, AI is a tool. The goal is not to "use AI" but to accomplish goals and objectives – or solve challenges – in new or better ways to achieve mission work more effectively.

When considering AI implementation, ask yourself a few questions first.

- How might this technology help us better serve our beneficiaries?
- Can AI help us solve a challenge or achieve a goal that was not previously possible, or do so better?
- Will it allow us to allocate our resources more efficiently and effectively?
- Does it align with our organizational values and priorities?

By clearly focusing on your mission, you can ensure that AI is a strategic asset rather than a distraction or a drain on resources. The goal is not to adopt AI for its own sake but to harness its potential to drive meaningful, positive change in the communities you serve.

As you embark on your AI journey, keep your mission at the heart of every decision and action. Continuously assess how AI can support your goals and be willing to adapt your approach as needed. By co-creating with AI in service of your mission, you can unlock new possibilities for impact and empower your nonprofit to make an even greater difference.

CLARIFICATION – WHAT EXACTLY ARE CHATBOTS?

People commonly think of chatbots as like the wildly popular generative AI (Gen AI) ChatGPT. Before ChatGPT, a chatbot may have been something you would think of as a support chat assistant on a website. There are many references in this book to chatbots, and there are a variety of types of chatbots, including:

1. "AI chatbots" (sometimes referred to in this book as "Gen AI chatbots") serve the purpose of facilitating conversational communication with AI. Enter a prompt into ChatGPT, Gemini, or Claude, and they will interact with a sophisticated language model or AI database to respond to your inquiry with that information.
2. Chatbots are also employed as virtual assistants for website support, helping in communication with site visitors.
3. Creating a custom chatbot can result in a personalized chat assistant on your website with your custom datasets or integrate with other AI applications as needed.

As you navigate the evolving landscape of AI, keep these perspectives in mind. Approach AI with a mix of optimism and caution, be mindful of the importance of effective prompting, learn from the experiences of others, and prioritize research and experimentation.

In conclusion, think of the hummingbird – a small, vibrant force of nature, darting through the air with unmatched speed and precision, its every action contributing to the health and growth of its ecosystem. This book aims to show how AI can be that hummingbird for your nonprofit. With its ability to swiftly analyze data, predict outcomes, and optimize strategies, AI can empower your organization to overcome challenges and achieve its mission more effectively. Just as the hummingbird's tireless efforts sustain the natural world, AI's capabilities can help sustain and amplify the impact of your nonprofit's work.

As you explore the chapters ahead, let the hummingbird image inspire you to embrace AI's potential to transform your vision into reality.

Note

1. Bernard Marr, "The Most Thought-Provoking Generative Artificial Intelligence Quotes of 2023," *Forbes*, November 29, 2023, https://www.forbes.com/sites/bernardmarr/2023/11/29/the-most-thought-provoking-generative-artificial-intelligence-quotes-of-2023/?sh=22bea0aa7afa.

CHAPTER 2

AI for Nonprofits

A I for nonprofits empowers leaders to unlock their potential to drive positive change. By exploring the various applications of AI in the nonprofit sector, we aim to demonstrate how this technology can help organizations become more effective, efficient, and impactful.

As Lotay Yang, a nonprofit leader, states, "Artificial intelligence may be able to help us be more effective in storytelling to facilitate better understanding, elicit empathy, and generate more ongoing support of what we do on a day-to-day basis helping people," a core component of success for many nonprofits that impacts many facets of their work.

Practical insights, real-world examples, and step-by-step guidance will:

1. Inspire nonprofit leaders to embrace and champion AI's adoption within their organizations, ensuring they do not get left behind in the digital age.
2. Highlight the benefits of AI for nonprofits, including increased efficiency, enhanced decision-making, and the ability to focus on higher-level tasks that maximize their unique human talents.

3. Provide strategies for leveraging AI to personalize messaging, streamline grant writing, and create compelling appeals that drive donor action and volunteer engagement.
4. Demonstrate how AI can help nonprofits analyze data, identify donor prospects, and optimize marketing efforts to improve targeting and increase return on investment (ROI).
5. Offer guidance on using AI to manage events, automate workflows, and reduce the stress and burden of routine tasks, allowing nonprofit professionals to focus on their cause and impact.

By exploring AI strengths and actionable insights, nonprofit leaders will have the knowledge and confidence to co-create with AI and achieve a profound impact in their communities and beyond.

Nonprofits' Missions and Critical Success Factors

Nonprofit organizations are vital in addressing societal issues and driving positive change. They serve as beacons of hope, illuminating our communities' most pressing challenges and working tirelessly to find solutions. From providing essential services to the most vulnerable populations to advocating for social justice and environmental sustainability, nonprofits are at the forefront of creating a better world for all.

Many of the ways AI can improve nonprofits internally can also improve the results of programs for beneficiaries. While AI can provide insights, ideas, and guidance based on data to help improve the job roles and environment for nonprofit staff, the same principles of enhancing the ability to create change can also benefit the community and the populations served.

"Across groups, a key strategy identified for strengthening the future workforce is to provide support systems and access to opportunities for those who are disadvantaged and lack work-based benefits. This includes removing barriers created by the lack of affordable and convenient transportation, childcare, housing, healthcare, food, and other basic needs. Not only can nonprofit organizations benefit from applying these insights to managing their own teams, but their missions often aim to provide these critical support services for the most vulnerable workers," explains Julie Maurer, PhD, of The Ohio State University.

EXAMPLES OF NONPROFIT MISSION AND PURPOSE

- **Poverty Alleviation:** Many nonprofits dedicate themselves to breaking the cycle of poverty by providing access to basic needs, education, and job training. They work to ensure that every individual can rise above their circumstances and build a brighter future.
- **Healthcare Access:** Nonprofits play a crucial role in ensuring everyone has access to quality healthcare regardless of socioeconomic status. They operate free clinics, provide health education, and advocate for health equity policies.
- **Environmental Conservation:** As the effects of climate change become increasingly apparent, nonprofits are taking charge of protecting our planet. They work to preserve natural habitats, promote sustainable practices, and educate the public about the importance of environmental stewardship.
- **Social Justice and Equality:** Nonprofits are at the forefront of the fight for social justice and equality. They work to combat discrimination, promote diversity and inclusion, and ensure that every individual has the right to live with dignity and respect.

OVERALL CHALLENGES

Despite their noble missions, nonprofits often navigate a complex landscape of challenges. Like a sailor trying to steer a ship through stormy seas, nonprofits must constantly adapt to changing circumstances while keeping their eye on the horizon.

- **Funding and Revenue:** Nonprofits often operate on tight budgets, relying heavily on donations and grants to fund their programs. Diversifying funding sources, managing administrative costs associated with grant funding, and exploring alternative types of funders, such as monthly recurring donors, can be ongoing challenges.
- **Leadership:** Utilizing AI's benefits is a leadership challenge, not just a technology challenge. Knowledge gaps or fears among leadership may hinder the adoption of innovative solutions. Leaders must drive change, align programs with the organization's mission, create a desired culture, develop strategic partnerships, and understand their impact on others.
- **Administrative Burden:** Nonprofits constantly strive to reduce administrative burdens to achieve a high return on their efforts. Streamlining processes and leveraging technology can help alleviate this challenge, which can also alleviate staff burnout.
- **Evolving Donor Landscape:** As the authors of *The Smart Nonprofit*, Beth Kanter and Allison Fine, note, nonprofits face the challenge of a "leaky bucket," where low donor retention rates create intense pressure for fundraisers as more donors leave even while new ones are added. Donors' interests and focus are changing, requiring nonprofits to address new ways to attract and retain donors while maintaining alignment with current supporters. Traditional approaches may need to be adapted to engage older and newer donors effectively.
- **Cross-Sector Collaboration:** Partnering with other nonprofits, governments, businesses, and community groups for collective impact is becoming increasingly important. Funders are shifting toward supporting collaborative

initiatives that unite organizations to accomplish shared goals.

- **Meeting Stakeholders Where They Are:** Nonprofits must understand their funders' different perspectives and needs. Framing the story and aligning requests with funders' priorities, such as asking for increased capacity to serve more people when seeking technology funding, can be more effective than simply requesting money for the technology itself.

- **Adapting Communication Strategies:** Nonprofits face the challenge of effectively communicating with internal and external stakeholders when changes occur. People must understand how they can benefit from and contribute to the organization's work. For example, when seeking volunteers, providing clear information on the website and developing systems to connect people with appropriate needs can foster a win-win situation for all involved.

- **Aligning Values and Communication:** Organizations must ensure that public communication accurately reflects their true values and mission. Shifting messaging across different channels, such as direct mail and email, to align with the organization's core values is essential for effective communication. It is also key to review various outreach methods regularly to see if they are current and if they would put your best foot forward if they were the only thing someone knew or saw about your nonprofit.

- **Cohesive Change Management:** When organizations have new divisions or initiatives, leadership must ensure that structural changes match the organization's overall needs. Cohesive change management is crucial for success.

- **Talent and Volunteer Acquisition:** Finding and attracting talented staff and volunteers is an ongoing challenge for nonprofits. Developing effective strategies to identify, engage, and retain skilled individuals is essential.

◆ **Adapting to AI:** As artificial intelligence becomes more prevalent, nonprofits must navigate the challenges of effectively incorporating AI into their operations and strategies.

CRITICAL SUCCESS FACTORS AND STRATEGIES

To navigate these challenges and achieve their missions, nonprofits must focus on several critical success factors:

1. **Partnerships:** By pooling resources and expertise, nonprofits can amplify their impact and achieve more than they could alone.

2. **Data-Driven Decision-Making:** Data-informed strategies and decisions give nonprofits that leverage this information a pronounced edge.

3. **Innovation and Adaptability:** A willingness to innovate and adapt to new challenges and opportunities is an asset now when technology is rapidly shifting.

4. **Stakeholder Engagement:** Nonprofits must prioritize building strong relationships with their stakeholders, including donors, volunteers, and the communities they serve.

5. **Leadership Development:** Investing in developing strong, adaptive, and visionary leaders is essential for nonprofits to navigate challenges and drive change effectively.

6. **Embracing Technology:** Leveraging the power of technology, nonprofits can work smarter and more efficiently toward their missions.

7. **Focusing on Diversity, Equity, and Inclusion (DEI):** Prioritizing DEI and creating a culture of belonging is the right thing to do and essential for building strong, resilient organizations.

By focusing on these critical success factors and embracing innovative strategies, nonprofits can overcome their challenges and continue to drive positive change. With dedication, resilience, a willingness to adapt, and the benefits of using AI, nonprofits can be an even more powerful force for good.

Critical Needs of Nonprofits Today and How AI Can Help

Nonprofit organizations face many pressing issues that require attention and innovative solutions, and AI is poised to help. As Leon Wilson of the Cleveland Foundation emphasizes, "Nonprofits must begin to engage with AI, adapting and innovating to meet their missions effectively in the face of critical challenges and needs."

HERE ARE THE TOP CRITICAL NEEDS THAT NONPROFITS MUST ADDRESS

"Responsible and ethical AI is the ambition for nonprofits. Generative AI democratizes AI. It makes innovation available to everyone, unlocking the potential of digital and human ingenuity together," states a research article from Avanade, a joint venture between Accenture and Microsoft that provides professional IT services. The report notes that nonprofits view improved efficiency as a primary first step for generative AI and that top priorities also include security and cyber resilience. Nonprofits also believe their beneficiaries want them to leverage emerging technologies like AI.[1]

- ◆ **Funding and Financial Stability:** Securing diverse and sustainable funding sources is a primary concern. Increasing competition for resources means organizations must explore innovative approaches to fundraising. AI-driven fundraising tools and transparent giving platforms using blockchain technology could offer potential solutions, enabling nonprofits to reach new donors, streamline the donation process, and build trust through enhanced transparency.

- **Impact Measurement and Reporting:** Demonstrating the effectiveness and impact of nonprofit programs is vital for securing funding and maintaining public trust. Utilizing AI to measure ROI and showcase impact through data-driven reports can strengthen accountability and attract support from donors and stakeholders. AI-powered analytics tools can help nonprofits identify key performance indicators, track progress, and communicate their impact more effectively. Outcomes are increasingly important to getting and keeping funding, and proving outcomes can be simplified with AI.

- **Volunteer Management:** Many nonprofits have difficulty recruiting, training, and retaining volunteers. AI-powered virtual assistants can enhance volunteer engagement by providing personalized support and guidance. Additionally, AI algorithms can match volunteers with opportunities that fit their skills and interests, making human resource allocation more efficient. These AI capabilities will be increasingly built into volunteer management and related systems. Since about 63 million people volunteer in the United States alone, and volunteering has many proven benefits related to health, happiness, and employment, it's a win-win anytime you can make it easier and more likely for someone wanting to volunteer to join your team.[2]

- **Diversity, Equity, and Inclusion (DEI):** Creating a diverse, equitable, and inclusive environment is essential for nonprofits to serve their communities and foster social change effectively. AI can assist in analyzing data to identify and address potential biases in programs and services, helping organizations ensure that their initiatives are accessible and beneficial to all. For example, AI can help process demographic data on program participants, like age, gender, race, ethnicity, and socioeconomic status, to identify any disparities in program participation and outcomes across different demographic groups. Internally, nonprofits can use AI to help with DEI by "analyzing recruitment processes, marketing campaigns, and internal communications to detect and reduce bias," a recent *Forbes* article suggests.[3]

◆ **Staff Recruitment and Retention:** Attracting and retaining qualified, passionate staff members is crucial for the success and sustainability of nonprofit organizations. Addressing burnout, workload, and competitive compensation is essential for creating a supportive and fulfilling work environment. Human resources (HR) professionals are already increasingly using AI creatively. Nonprofit HR's 2023 Pulse Survey noted many aspects of the HR process are being augmented by AI, like administrative tasks, policy drafting, rewriting job descriptions, bias checking, creating interview questions, and more.[4]

◆ **Marketing and Communication:** Effectively communicating the nonprofit's mission, impact, and value to the public is vital for building awareness, garnering support, and driving engagement.

The 2023 Nonprofit Tech for Good Report, findings noted as follows, highlights how important digital outreach is to nonprofits, for example – and AI can help craft more persuasive, inspiring, and customized messaging for all digital channels.

The 20 most effective digital marketing and fundraising tools according to 1,049 nonprofit digital marketers and fundraisers, 2023[5]

1. Website – 84%

2. Social Media – 65%

3. Email Newsletters – 64%

4. Email fundraising appeals – 43%

5. Monthly giving programs – 37%

6. Social media advertising – 31%
7. Peer-to-peer-fundraising – 29%
8. Customer Relationship Management (CRM) software – 24%
9. Virtual fundraising events – 23%
10. #GivingTuesday – 22%
11. Video – 21%
12. Tribute giving programs – 19%
13. Presenting webinars – 17%
14. Cause awareness days – 17%
15. Crowdfunding – 15%
16. Infographics – 15%
17. Blogging – 11%
18. Search engine advertising – 10%
19. Online fundraising auctions – 9%
20. Web-based annual reports – 9%

AI-powered social media automation tools can help non-profits optimize their online presence, reach wider audiences, and deliver personalized content to supporters. Additionally, AI algorithms can analyze supporter data to identify key demographics, preferences, and behaviors, enabling targeted and effective communication strategies.

- ◆ **Partnerships and Collaboration:** Building strategic partnerships and fostering collaboration within the nonprofit sector is key to achieving systemic change and maximizing impact. Collaborative AI development initiatives and community-driven AI innovation can facilitate resource sharing, knowledge exchange, and collective problem-solving. By working together and leveraging AI technologies, nonprofits can tackle complex social issues more effectively and create lasting, transformative change. It may be possible for multiple organizations to share mutually beneficial technology or data resources, for example, or use AI to determine strengths among large working groups to divide grants or projects in ways that make the most of all available resources.

♦ **Ethical Considerations and Responsible AI Implementation:** As nonprofits adopt AI, addressing ethical concerns and responsible data use is crucial. Organizations must consider risks like privacy breaches, bias, and job displacement. Balancing AI benefits with these risks ensures sustainable use. Developing strong ethical frameworks and governance structures guides AI initiatives to align with nonprofit values and promote the greater good. Many helpful resources are available because this is an area of critical concern to all nonprofits.

Global Giving, for example, provides guidance and ideas for getting started, including tips on modeling existing examples like Fundraising.ai's Framework toward Responsible and Beneficial AI for Fundraising,[6] developing initial policies, thoroughly vetting AI vendors, training staff and board members, informing donors and collecting consent, and maintaining a strict model and data hygiene routine.[7]

♦ **Impact on Cause or Community Served:** AI offers huge potential to enhance impact and better serve communities. Organizations can gain deep insights into people's needs and challenges using AI-powered tools for data analysis, predictive modeling, and personalized service delivery. This leads to targeted interventions, optimized resources, and tailored support. By spotting trends and predicting future demands, AI ensures programs stay relevant.

♦ **Security, Privacy, and Cybersecurity:** As nonprofits increasingly rely on digital technologies and data-driven approaches, ensuring the security and privacy of sensitive information becomes a critical concern. Cybersecurity threats such as data breaches, hacking attempts, and phishing scams pose significant risks to nonprofit organizations, potentially compromising donor trust and financial stability. AI-powered security solutions can help nonprofits detect and prevent cyber threats, monitor network activity, and protect sensitive data from unauthorized access. By leveraging AI for cybersecurity, nonprofits can safeguard their digital assets, maintain the confidentiality of supporter information, and build a robust and resilient infrastructure to support their missions in the digital age.

The National Council of Nonprofits offers an excellent review of the topic along with resources. Key recommendations include conducting risk assessments to inventory and secure sensitive data, understanding legal obligations related to personally identifiable information (PII), using frameworks like National Institute of Standards and Technology (NIST) for risk management, and considering cyber liability insurance.[8]

By addressing these top critical needs, nonprofit organizations can position themselves for success. Strategically and responsibly embracing AI technologies can enable nonprofits to enhance their impact, drive innovation, and build a more sustainable and equitable future.

Revolutionizing Altruism

Altruism, the selfless concern for others' well-being, is at the heart of nonprofit work. By being in or involved with the nonprofit sector, you have already chosen an altruistic approach to life. Nonprofits have unprecedented opportunities to amplify their impact and achieve their missions more effectively by co-creating and innovating with AI. By leveraging the power of artificial intelligence, organizations can tackle complex challenges, optimize their operations, and deliver personalized experiences to their stakeholders.

AI can help nonprofits unlock new possibilities, overcome challenges, and accelerate their altruistic missions. AI technologies can supercharge altruistic efforts, extending reach, deepening impact, and creating lasting change. This is the power of AI – to produce more world-changing differences faster. Because as Jane Goodall stated eloquently, "What you do makes a difference. And you have to decide what kind of difference you want to make." Here are a few ways AI can change nonprofits for the better.

DEMOCRATIZING ACCESS

The advent of generative AI tools and applications has democratized access to cutting-edge technology, empowering nonprofits to develop tailored solutions with AI applications that address their unique needs. By harnessing these tools, organizations can streamline their workflows, automate repetitive tasks, and generate valuable insights from their data.

- New generative AI tools and applications enable end users to create customized solutions. Top Generative AI Tool Overview has many listed.[9]
- Through the use of AI, nonprofits can create a vision and plan to address existing problems and challenges.
- AI can help solve problems, increase efficiency, and expand reach across various domains (e.g. administration, fundraising, communications, marketing).

OPTIMIZING AI'S TRANSFORMATIVE POTENTIAL IN NONPROFIT WORK

Leveraging AI technologies, nonprofits can optimize their resource allocation, personalize their engagement strategies, and predict future trends to stay ahead of the curve. For example, the International Committee of the Red Cross (http://ICRC.org) used machine learning to optimize humanitarian aid allocation.[10]

As noted in an article on ReliefWeb.int., "Artificial Intelligence (AI) has the potential to reshape the way we respond and coordinate humanitarian response – helping humanitarians offer more efficient and effective ways to deliver aid and support to people in need. The UN General Assembly's draft resolution recognizes that safe, secure, and trustworthy AI can contribute to the 17 Sustainable Development Goals and 'promote digital transformation; promote peace; overcome digital divides between and within countries; and promote and protect the enjoyment of human rights and fundamental freedoms for all.'"[11]

- ◆ Streamline operations, generate valuable insights, and enhance personalized engagement.
- ◆ Automate inefficient processes, analyze vast amounts of data, personalize communication, and predict future trends.

STREAMLINING THE EVALUATION AND MITIGATION OF RISKS

To ensure successful AI integration, nonprofits must prioritize data security and privacy, implement responsible data management practices, and invest in staff training.

- ◆ Carefully evaluate options and consider potential risks and benefits.
- ◆ Developing customized AI applications may not be practical or feasible for smaller organizations.
- ◆ Leverage existing AI-powered tools and platforms for a more accessible and cost-effective entry point.
- ◆ Prioritize data security and privacy, ensuring responsible data management practices.
- ◆ Invest in staff training and development to foster AI literacy and empower employees

LEVERAGING AI IN MARKETING AND COMMUNICATIONS

AI-powered marketing and communication strategies can help nonprofits reach wider audiences, engage supporters more effectively, and deliver personalized experiences. By leveraging natural language processing and machine learning algorithms, organizations can analyze supporter preferences, tailor their messaging, and optimize their outreach efforts across various channels.

- Enhance outreach efforts through personalized email campaigns, targeted social media advertising, chatbots, and virtual assistants.
- Leverage natural language processing and machine learning algorithms to tailor messaging, anticipate supporter preferences, and deliver relevant content.

FOSTERING A CULTURE OF INNOVATION

Fostering a culture of innovation and providing resources for AI literacy can help nonprofits adopt new solutions only available through AI technologies.

- Approach AI with a strategic and informed mindset.
- Carefully plan initiatives, evaluate potential risks and benefits, and prioritize data security and privacy.
- Capitalize on the new capabilities AI brings to the table, which will be noted in detail in the following chapters.

AI revolutionizes the nonprofit sector by enhancing efficiency, decision-making, and impact. It highlights nonprofit leaders' need to embrace AI to avoid being left behind in the digital age, emphasizing the technology's benefits in personalizing messaging, streamlining operations, and optimizing resource allocation. Broader challenges nonprofits face, such as funding, leadership, administrative burdens, and evolving donor landscapes, call for AI-driven strategies to overcome these obstacles. By fostering collaboration, data-driven decision-making, innovation, stakeholder engagement, leadership development, and a focus on diversity, equity, and inclusion, nonprofits can leverage AI to amplify their mission and drive profound positive change in their communities.

Notes

1. Avanade, "Generative AI Readiness Report: Nonprofit AI Report," accessed December 14, 2023, https://www.avanade .com/en/insights/generative-ai-readiness-report/nonprofit-ai-report.

2. Double the Donation, "Volunteer Statistics," accessed December 14, 2023, https://doublethedonation.com/volunteer-statistics.

3. Jia Wertz, "How AI Can Be Leveraged for Diversity and Inclusion," *Forbes*, November 19, 2023, https://www.forbes.com/sites/jiawertz/2023/11/19/how-ai-can-be-leveraged-for-diversity-and-inclusion/?sh=3501d244ee9e.

4. Nonprofit HR, "2023 Social Impact AI Survey," accessed December 14, 2023, https://www.nonprofithr.com/wp-content/uploads/2023/09/2023-Social-Impact-AI-Survey_Nonprofit-HR.pdf.

5. *Nonprofit Tech for Good: The Digital Marketing & Fundraising Report*, 2023, accessed December 14, 2023, https://www.nptechforgood.com/wp-content/uploads/2023/02/Nonprofit-Tech-for-Good-Report-Final2-2023.pdf.

6. Fundraising.AI, "Framework toward Responsible and Beneficial AI for Fundraising," accessed December 14, 2023, https://fundraising.ai/framework.

7. Global Giving, "Nonprofit Responsible AI Use Policies," accessed December 14, 2023, https://www.globalgiving.org/learn/nonprofit-responsible-ai-use-policies.

8. National Council of Nonprofits, "Cybersecurity for Nonprofits," accessed December 14, 2023, https://www.councilofnonprofits.org/running-nonprofit/administration-and-financial-management/cybersecurity-nonprofits.

9. David Needle, "Top Generative AI App & Tool Overview," *eWeek*, November 27, 2023, https://www.eweek.com/artificial-intelligence/generative-ai-apps-tools.

10. Anne-Marie Bujard, "Harnessing the Potential of Artificial Intelligence for Humanitarian Action," *International Review of the Red Cross* 99, no. 903 (2017): 421–449, https://international-review.icrc.org/articles/harnessing-the-potential-of-artificial-intelligence-for-humanitarian-action-919.

11. ReliefWeb, "Artificial Intelligence in Humanitarian Action," accessed December 14, 2023, https://reliefweb.int/blogpost/artificial-intelligence-humanitarian-action-new-topics-page-reliefweb.

CHAPTER 3

World-Changing Emergence of AI and How It Impacts Nonprofits

As AI continues to advance and affect many business and life functions, it presents challenges and opportunities for nonprofit organizations. Leaders in this sector must navigate this evolving landscape, addressing concerns while harnessing AI's potential to amplify their impact and achieve their missions more effectively.

Global Impact Needs Outlined in the United Nations Sustainable Development Goals

When considering the global impact of AI on nonprofits, it is interesting to look at the globally established universal framework for action to protect the planet, fight inequality, and end extreme poverty by 2030: The United Nations (UN) Sustainable Development Goals (SDGs).[1] These 17 goals address global challenges, including poverty, inequality, climate change, environmental degradation, peace, and justice.

The United Nations Sustainable Development Goals, Wikimedia via http://
UN.org, provided as public information material designed primarily to inform
the public about United Nations activities.[2]

The 17 United Nations Sustainable Development Goals (UN SDGs)

1. **No Poverty:** End poverty in all its forms everywhere.
2. **Zero Hunger:** End hunger, achieve food security and improved nutrition, and promote sustainable agriculture.
3. **Good Health and Well-Being:** Ensure healthy lives and promote well-being for all at all ages.
4. **Quality Education:** Ensure inclusive and equitable quality education and promote lifelong learning opportunities for all.
5. **Gender Equality:** Achieve gender equality and empower all women and girls.
6. **Clean Water and Sanitation:** Ensure availability and sustainable management of water and sanitation for all.
7. **Affordable and Clean Energy:** Ensure access to affordable, reliable, sustainable, and modern energy for all.

8. **Decent Work and Economic Growth:** Promote sustained, inclusive, and sustainable economic growth, full and productive employment, and decent work for all.

9. **Industry, Innovation, and Infrastructure:** Build resilient infrastructure, promote inclusive and sustainable industrialization, and foster innovation.

10. **Reduced Inequalities:** Reduce inequality within and among countries.

11. **Sustainable Cities and Communities:** Make cities and human settlements inclusive, safe, resilient, and sustainable.

12. **Responsible Consumption and Production:** Ensure sustainable consumption and production patterns.

13. **Climate Action:** Take urgent action to combat climate change and its impacts.

14. **Life Below Water:** Conserve and sustainably use the oceans, seas, and marine resources for sustainable development.

15. **Life on Land:** Protect, restore, and promote sustainable use of terrestrial ecosystems, sustainably manage forests, combat desertification, halt and reverse land degradation, and halt biodiversity loss.

16. **Peace, Justice, and Strong Institutions:** Promote peaceful and inclusive societies for sustainable development, provide access to justice for all and build effective, accountable, and inclusive institutions at all levels.

17. **Partnerships for the Goals:** Strengthen the means of implementation and revitalize the global partnership for sustainable development, which includes finance, technology, capacity-building, trade, policy and institutional coherence, multi-stakeholder partnerships, and data, monitoring, and accountability.

These 17 goals collectively address some of the world's most pressing challenges. Therefore, considering these global challenges, the question is how can AI help nonprofit organizations approach and solve these and other important goals?

AI Impact, Concerns, and Opportunities

Broadly speaking, many people with experience with AI and other technologies over long periods view AI as an asset, and something that if used correctly, can augment human capabilities with additional time, the ability to complete tasks a human cannot, and overall time savings. Here, we will discuss several facets of AI, mostly positive, with some current shortcomings and things to be mindful of. As former CEO of IBM Ginni Rometty puts it:

> Some people call this artificial intelligence, but the reality is this technology will enhance us. So instead of artificial intelligence, I think we'll augment our intelligence.[3]

Job Security Concerns and the Potential for Augmentation

Robin Bordoli, partner at Authentic Ventures, has framed the question about how AI might impact jobs like this:

> I think what makes AI different from other technologies is that it's going to bring humans and machines closer together. AI is sometimes incorrectly framed as machines replacing humans. It's not about machines replacing humans, but machines augmenting humans.[4]

One of the primary fears surrounding AI right now is the potential for job displacement. As AI technologies become increasingly sophisticated, there is a growing apprehension that they may replace human workers in various roles. This concern extends to fundraising, grant writing, marketing, and communication within the nonprofit sector. However, rather than viewing AI as a threat, nonprofit leaders should approach it as an opportunity to augment and enhance human capabilities. By learning about AI and incorporating it strategically into their organizations, nonprofits can plan to co-create with AI, leveraging its benefits while ensuring that staff members remain engaged and valued contributors. In this way, an organization could see gains in innovation and impact as staff free up time for strategic thinking, creativity, personal interactions with stakeholders, and other uniquely human talents.

Administrative Efficiency Unlocked

As previously noted, AI's vast and varied opportunities include streamlining processes, saving time, and allocating resources more effectively through efficient data analysis, identifying patterns, and generating insights that inform decision-making and strategy. AI can help automate repetitive tasks, freeing staff time for more creative and impactful work.

Why does this matter? The hope is that there will be more time for uniquely human creativity, innovation, and inspiration, which can lead to leaps forward and connect people more deeply.

And as Dr. Kai-Fu Lee, chairman and CEO, Sinovation Ventures notes:

> Humans need and want more time to interact with each other. I think AI coming about and replacing routine jobs is pushing us to do what we should be doing anyway: the creation of more humanistic service jobs.[5]

Strategic AI Integration and Robust Data Management

Nonprofits that embrace AI and integrate it strategically into their operations will likely achieve their goals faster and more efficiently. However, this adoption requires careful consideration of data security and privacy. Organizations must establish robust data management practices and ensure that sensitive information is protected and handled with the utmost care. Furthermore, nonprofits may need to invest in staff training and development to build the necessary skills and knowledge to work seamlessly alongside AI technologies.

Clem Delangue, co-founder and CEO of Hugging Face, explains, "I think trust comes from transparency and control. You want to see the datasets that these models have been trained on. You want to see how this model has been built, what kind of biases it includes. That's how you can trust the system. It's really hard to trust something that you don't understand."[6] Transparency in AI is valuable internally and externally, and strong policies regarding data are, too.

Empowering Fundraising Efforts and Diversifying Funding Sources

One of the primary challenges facing nonprofits today is securing sustainable funding. AI can be crucial in diversifying funding sources and identifying new opportunities. For instance, AI-powered smart grant matching platforms can help nonprofits find and apply for relevant grants more efficiently, often even proactively and automatically (see "Case Study – Grant Development" in Chapter 5).

AI can also assist in generating compelling content for fundraising campaigns and marketing materials, enhancing the organization's ability to attract and retain donors while ensuring consistent messaging and brand alignment. Additionally, AI can help understand donor patterns and trends, enabling nonprofits to tailor their fundraising efforts and engage with supporters more effectively, particularly as donor demographics shift with the rise of Generation Z.

Innovative Leadership: Embracing AI as a Catalyst for Change and Alleviating Staff Burnout through Intelligent Automation

Leadership plays a pivotal role in successfully adopting AI within nonprofit organizations. Leaders who embrace change by removing barriers and fostering an environment encouraging innovation and thoughtful experimentation can empower their teams to leverage AI effectively. AI can enable nonprofits to achieve a higher return on their efforts, mitigate staff burnout, and give teams time to explore new possibilities and fresh ideas.

Donor Behavior Analysis: Adapting to Evolving Preferences

Particularly with the rise of Generation Z, nonprofits need ways of engaging and communicating with supporters as donor demographics shift. AI can help organizations understand and respond to these changing preferences, such as accepting cryptocurrency donations or leveraging digital touchpoints for storytelling. Utilizing AI to gain insights into donor behavior and preferences, nonprofits can tailor their approaches and build stronger relationships with their supporters.

Fostering Collaboration for Collective Impact

AI can make a significant impact by joining the strengths of many organizations toward one collective goal. Nonprofits often benefit from partnering with other nonprofit organizations, government entities, businesses, and community and faith-based groups to achieve collective impact.

For example, as Sopact highlights, "The Chicago Literacy Alliance is an association of more than 100 organizations helping to meet the literacy needs of people of all ages and backgrounds. This collective impact initiative brings together a network of organizations to collaborate on projects, share resources, and generate new ideas to increase literacy rates in the Chicago area."[7]

AI can facilitate this process by identifying collaborators with similar goals and missions. By analyzing data from various public sources, such as Form 990s, annual reports, and website content, AI can help nonprofits find the right partners to foster meaningful collaborations.

Optimizing Communications

Effective communication is essential for nonprofits to engage with their stakeholders, including internal staff, external communities, funders, volunteers, donors, and the people they serve. AI can help organizations tailor their communications to address the specific needs of each group. Through techniques like prompt engineering, AI can generate targeted and personalized messages, ensuring consistency and clarity across all communication channels.

Agility in Adapting to Challenges

When new challenges arise, nonprofits need to adapt and change. AI can support organizations in this process by providing insights, generating roadmaps, and creating checklists to guide decision-making. By leveraging AI to analyze data and identify trends, nonprofits can respond more quickly to emerging needs and opportunities.

Optimizing Human Resources and Volunteer Management

Talent acquisition and volunteer management are critical components of nonprofit success. AI can streamline these processes by matching volunteers with suitable opportunities based on their skills and interests. Additionally, AI can help organizations analyze and optimize their hiring processes, from ensuring that job postings are unbiased and don't contain unnecessary requirements to suggesting diverse and inclusive job sites to post positions that reach a diverse range of candidates.

Many specifically focused job boards with audiences that may not always be found on the large and broad job boards exist. Diversity for Social Impact has an excellent introduction to hiring inclusion and resources to help find Black professionals, Indigenous professionals, and other BIPOC (Black, Indigenous, People of Color) minority professionals, people with disabilities or chronic illnesses, LGBTQIA+ (Lesbian, Gay, Bisexual, Transgender, Queer, Intersex, and Asexual; "+" represents other identities that may be part of the community, such as pansexual, agender, non-binary, gender fluid, and allies of the community) professionals, senior retired or semi-retirement professionals, and many more.[8]

Investing in Training and Continuous Learning

To fully enjoy AI's benefits, nonprofits need comprehensive AI development plans and investment in staff training. This includes providing AI training courses and creating a culture of continuous learning. However, organizations must also be cautious about uploading proprietary information, such as donor lists or intellectual property, to AI systems to mitigate the risk of data breaches.

Promoting Diversity, Equity, and Inclusion (DEI)

Finally, AI can promote diversity, equity, and inclusion (DEI) within nonprofit organizations. AI can identify potential biases and suggest improvements by reviewing policies, processes, hiring practices, and communication materials. This helps nonprofits create an inclusive environment and effectively serve their diverse communities. However, all policy recommendations or materials should be reviewed by adept humans with deep knowledge and subject matter expertise to avoid inadvertent mistakes.

AI provides unique opportunities to shape the nonprofit sector's future and drive positive change by amplifying impact, achieving missions more effectively, and confidently navigating the changing landscape strategically and responsibly.

The Current State of AI Usage in the Nonprofit Sector

AI ADOPTION IN THE NONPROFIT SECTOR: A GRADUAL YET TRANSFORMATIVE JOURNEY

Integrating AI into the nonprofit realm has been a steady, albeit gradual, process. While adoption rates have lagged behind other sectors, according to a 2024 Google.org study,[9] more than half of nonprofits are already using AI for some tasks. As AI capabilities continue to advance and costs become more accessible, nonprofits are well-positioned to accelerate their AI deployment significantly in the forthcoming years.

LEVERAGING AI FOR ENHANCED FUNDRAISING INITIATIVES

Fundraising efforts are one of the primary areas where nonprofits harness AI's power. Generative AI techniques enable organizations to analyze donor data and predict giving patterns, facilitating the development of highly targeted and effective fundraising campaigns. By integrating AI-powered chatbots and AI-driven analytics into their operations, nonprofits can enhance communication channels and gain invaluable insights. Automating repetitive back-office tasks or conducting rapid donor data analysis can alleviate staff from manual workloads and elevate the efficacy of fundraising outreach strategies.

DATA-DRIVEN DECISION-MAKING

AI is also pivotal in empowering nonprofits to make informed, data-driven decisions. Predictive analytics equip organizations with the capability to forecast needs and refine donor communication strategies. By analyzing historical contribution patterns, nonprofits can target the most suitable donors more efficiently. This aspect holds particular significance as donors increasingly demand tangible evidence of the impact of their contributions, compelling nonprofits to demonstrate measurable results and effective resource allocation.

UNLOCKING ADDITIONAL BENEFITS
Beyond fundraising and decision-making, AI offers many additional benefits to nonprofits. Machine learning, a subset of AI, enables computers to learn from data and continuously enhance their performance over time. This capability can be leveraged to automate repetitive tasks, such as data entry and analysis, freeing up staff time to focus on more strategic endeavors. Moreover, AI can significantly improve the accuracy and speed of tasks like donor segmentation and marketing campaigns.

ENGAGEMENT AND PERSONALIZED SUPPORTER EXPERIENCES
Moreover, AI-powered chatbots and other interactive tools can facilitate meaningful engagement with supporters and provide personalized experiences. For example, a chatbot can promptly address common inquiries about an organization's cause or assist donors in making contributions. This heightened level of engagement can foster stronger relationships with supporters and ultimately drive a more significant impact.[10]

CHALLENGES OF IMPLEMENTING AI IN NONPROFITS
While AI presents numerous opportunities for nonprofits, its implementation is not without challenges. One of the primary concerns is the cost associated with adopting AI technology. Although costs are anticipated to decrease as AI becomes more prevalent, nonprofits may initially face resource constraints when allocating funds for AI investments. Thinking about AI as helping to increase capacity when requesting funding, versus requesting funding for AI technology itself, is more likely to lead to funding.

Reviewing the following key areas for capacity-building grants as discussed on The Grantsmanship Center, AI fits nicely into several and should be framed as such.

Relevant requests for a capacity-building grant proposal:

- **Strategic planning** to guide organizational development and services for a two- to five-year period.
- **A database system** to efficiently capture and organize data on service delivery and outcomes.
- **A fund development plan** to help diversify and expand funding streams.
- **Upgraded technology** to enable staff to work more efficiently.
- **A volunteer management system** to support service provision in a cost-effective way.
- **Succession planning** when long-term leadership is close to retirement.
- **Exploration of mergers** when combining two nonprofits could result in increased stability, cost efficiencies, or service reach.[11]

ETHICAL CONSIDERATIONS

Ethical concerns surrounding AI, such as bias and fairness, must be carefully addressed, and nonprofits should remain vigilant. They should take proactive steps to ensure their AI systems are transparent and accountable. Privacy and security risks are also crucial considerations, underscoring the necessity for organizations to collect and utilize data ethically and securely to maintain the trust of their stakeholders.

ESTABLISHING SAFEGUARDS AND GUIDELINES

To navigate these challenges and harness AI's full potential, nonprofits must establish robust safeguards and ethical guidelines for responsible utilization and governance. This includes developing comprehensive policies for the responsible use of AI to maintain trust and transparency across all operations.

AMPLIFYING IMPACT WITH RESPONSIBLE ADOPTION

As AI continues to evolve and become increasingly accessible, nonprofits have a unique opportunity to leverage this technology to amplify their impact and achieve their missions more effectively. By strategically incorporating AI into their operations, organizations can streamline processes, make data-driven decisions, and engage supporters in innovative and meaningful ways. However, nonprofits must approach AI adoption responsibly, address ethical concerns, and ensure that the technology is utilized to benefit the communities they serve.

GROWING RECOGNITION OF AI'S VALUE

The potential of artificial intelligence (AI) in the nonprofit sector is undeniable, and forward-thinking organizations are actively exploring ways to harness its power. While adopting AI within the nonprofit realm has been gradual, many organizations recognize its value in driving productivity and amplifying impact. As more organizations recognize the value of AI and invest in its implementation, we can anticipate a significant surge in AI adoption across the sector. This shift is already evidenced by a 2024 *Forbes* study:

Metric	Percentage
Organizations that believe AI would boost productivity	89%
Organizations actively utilizing AI technologies	28%
Nonprofits actively leveraging AI tools	23%
Nonprofits that believe AI innovation aligns with their core values	73%
Nonprofit leaders who find AI has the potential to make their work more efficient and impactful	75%

Source: "AI and Nonprofits: Not If or When, But How," Forbes.[12]

These statistics highlight a burgeoning interest in and acceptance of AI within the sector as nonprofit leaders increasingly recognize its potential. While challenges remain, such as resource constraints and ethical considerations, the nonprofit community is actively exploring strategies to integrate AI responsibly into operations.

Potential Impact on Populations Served by Nonprofits

The nonprofit sector is constantly evolving, with it, the tools and technologies available to organizations working to make a difference. AI technology has immense potential to revolutionize how nonprofits operate and serve their communities. Silvio Savarese, executive vice president and chief scientist, Salesforce AI Research says,

> I've long believed that AI won't just enhance the way we live but transform it fundamentally . . . AI is placing tools of unprecedented power, flexibility, and even personalization into everyone's hands, requiring little more than natural language to operate. They'll assist us in many parts of our lives, taking on the role of superpowered collaborators.[13]

VULNERABLE POPULATIONS

AI can be used to develop targeted interventions for vulnerable populations, such as those experiencing homelessness, poverty, or food insecurity. AI-powered tools can also help connect individuals with needed resources and services.

PEOPLE WITH DISABILITIES

AI can be used to innovate or help develop technologies that empower people with disabilities to live more independent and fulfilling lives. Additionally, AI-powered tools can help break down communication barriers and promote inclusion. The World Economic Forum noted, "Generative AI can support people with disabilities by fueling existing assistive technology and robotics, learning, accommodation and accessibility solutions."[14]

CHILDREN AND YOUTH

AI can be used to create personalized learning experiences or tutoring that cater to individual needs and learning styles or to identify and address mental health challenges among children and youth.

CHALLENGES AND SOLUTIONS TO ACCESSIBILITY AND AFFORDABILITY OF AI

AI technology can be expensive and difficult to implement, but it doesn't have to be. It can also significantly impact nonprofits' operations and service to their communities. Let's explore ways to make AI accessible and affordable for nonprofit organizations.

In addition to always checking a product website to see if free or discounted nonprofit plans exist, you can contact companies directly and ask if they can give you a nonprofit discount. You may be asked to provide documentation; companies often provide nonprofit discounts even if they are not published on their sites.

Additionally, many software and services providers in the non-profit space regularly publish posts, webinars, or resources about categories of free or inexpensive and valuable AI tools, including the following, and many others:

- ◆ DonorBox[15]
- ◆ Funraise[16]
- ◆ Whole Whale[17]
- ◆ Wild Apricot[18]

Large tech companies often have special programs, discounts, tools, or resources for nonprofits as well.

Responsible AI use can tap into the power to improve efficiency, personalize interventions, and reach more people to serve. However, it is important to address the challenges associated with AI, such as data privacy, content accuracy, bias, and accessibility, to ensure that its use benefits all populations served by nonprofits.

Benefits of AI and How Generative AI Can Accelerate the Critical Needs Solutions for Nonprofits Today

As nonprofit organizations grapple with pressing challenges that demand innovative responses, AI emerges as a transformative tool to address critical needs and drive profound impact. By strategically leveraging AI, nonprofits can optimize their operations, enhance fundraising efforts, and amplify their mission-driven work.

1. **Optimizing Fundraising Strategies with AI**

    AI-powered tools can revolutionize how nonprofits approach fundraising, enabling them to make data-driven decisions and personalize their outreach efforts.

    • Utilize AI to analyze vast datasets and develop targeted, personalized communication strategies.

    • Identify the most effective messaging for different donor segments to boost engagement and campaign success.

    • Employ AI-driven tools to streamline donor data analysis and uncover insights for improved donor retention.

2. **Streamlining Research and Grant Applications**

    Generative AI can significantly reduce the time and effort required for researching and applying for grants, allowing nonprofits to focus on their core mission.

    • Integrate databases and harness AI's analytical capabilities to compare funding opportunities efficiently.

    • Leverage Generative AI to analyze grant patterns, offer insights, and recommend new opportunities aligned with the nonprofit's goals.

    • Automate repetitive tasks in the grant application process, allowing staff to focus on mission-critical activities.

3. **Addressing Leadership and Administrative Challenges**

    AI can help nonprofit leaders navigate complex challenges by providing data-driven insights and automating administrative tasks, enabling them to focus on strategic decision-making.

- Strategically plan AI integration, assign clear roles, and ensure the organization and staff are prepared for new workflows.
- Utilize AI to reduce the burden of administrative tasks, preventing burnout and enhancing job satisfaction.

Allison Fine, president of Every.org, states, "Hopefully, AI will absorb tasks that people do not enjoy or that are 'time-consuming,'" and leaders will channel this newfound time not into doing more of the same things but into doing things differently with new tools.

4. **Enhancing Recruitment and Reducing Bias**

AI-powered recruitment tools can help nonprofits identify the best candidates while minimizing biases, ensuring a diverse and inclusive workforce.

- Leverage AI to tailor job postings more precisely and assess candidates fairly, focusing on relevant qualifications.
- Anonymize applications using AI to eliminate biases in the hiring process.
- Utilize generative AI to standardize recruitment criteria, ensuring a fair and objective selection process.

5. **Supporting Diversity, Equity, and Inclusion (DEI)**

AI can assist nonprofits in creating inclusive environments by generating unbiased policies and materials that reflect diverse perspectives.

- Employ AI to assist in drafting policies that promote inclusiveness and are free of biases.
- Generate materials that reflect diverse perspectives and adopt practices that enhance cultural competence.
- Implement safeguards to prevent inherent biases within AI technologies from affecting decision-making processes.

6. **Optimizing Communication and Marketing Efforts**

Generative AI can help nonprofit marketers craft compelling and consistent marketing faster and easier, in more customized ways, to create messages that resonate with their target audience and align with their mission.

- Utilize generative AI to develop consistent and impactful marketing messages aligned with the organization's core values and mission.
- Personalize engagement at all contact points, including content creation, email marketing, and social media marketing.
- Adapt communication strategies based on emerging trends identified through AI analysis.

7. Improving Donor Engagement and Retention

Cultivating strong relationships with existing donors is crucial for long-term sustainability. AI can provide valuable insights into donor preferences and behaviors, enabling nonprofits to personalize engagement strategies and maximize donor lifetime value.

- Leverage AI-driven tools to analyze donor data and identify patterns in giving behavior, preferences, and engagement levels.
- Utilize AI to segment donors based on their giving history, interests, and engagement patterns, enabling personalized communication and tailored stewardship strategies.
- Implement AI-powered chatbots or virtual assistants to provide instant support to donors, answer questions, and offer personalized recommendations.

AI offers unprecedented opportunities to optimize operations, enhance fundraising efforts, and amplify impact. By co-creating with AI, nonprofits can unlock new possibilities, overcome challenges, and accelerate their mission-driven work. As Allison Fine from Every.org emphasizes, embracing AI is a leadership challenge rather than solely a technological one. Nonprofit leaders can take advantage of AI's power by strategically planning AI integration, assigning clear roles, and preparing their organizations for new workflows.

Notes

1. United Nations, "The 17 Goals," *United Nations Sustainable Development Goals*, accessed August 1, 2023, https://sdgs.un.org/goals.
2. Wikimedia, "Sustainable Development Goals," *Wikimedia Commons*, accessed August 1, 2023, https://commons.wikimedia.org/wiki/File:Sustainable_Development_Goals.png.
3. Bernard Marr, "28 Best Quotes About Artificial Intelligence." *Bernard Marr & Co.*, June 26, 2023, https://bernardmarr.com/28-best-quotes-about-artificial-intelligence.
4. Salesforce, "The Best AI Quotes from Experts," *Salesforce*, accessed August 1, 2023, https://www.salesforce.com/blog/ai-quotes.
5. Salesforce, "The Best AI Quotes from Experts."
6. Salesforce, "The Best AI Quotes from Experts."
7. Sopact, "Collective Impact: What It Is and How to Do It Well," *Sopact*, accessed August 1, 2023, https://www.sopact.com/guides/collective-impact.
8. Diversity. Social, "Diversity and Inclusion Job Boards," *Diversity. Social*, accessed August 1, 2023, https://diversity.social/diversity-inclusion-job-boards.
9. Kevin Flanigan, "More Than Half of Nonprofits Use AI, Google.org Survey Finds," *Philanthropy*, January 11, 2024, https://www.philanthropy.com/article/more-than-half-of-nonprofits-use-a-i-google-org-survey-finds.
10. Funraise, "Why Your Nonprofit's Website Needs a Chatbot," *Funraise*, accessed August 1, 2023, https://www.funraise.org/blog/why-your-nonprofits-website-needs-a-chatbot.
11. The Grantsmanship Center, "Understanding Capacity-Building Grant Proposals," *The Grantsmanship Center*, August 11, 2020, https://www.tgci.com/blog/2020/08/understanding-capacity-building-grant-proposals.
12. Forbes Nonprofit Council, "AI and Nonprofits: Not If or When, But How," *Forbes*, September 27, 2023, https://www.forbes.com/sites/forbesnonprofitcouncil/2023/09/27/ai-and-nonprofits-not-if-or-when-but-how.

13. Salesforce, "The Best AI Quotes from Experts."

14. World Economic Forum, "Generative AI Holds Potential for People with Disabilities – If Developed Responsibly," *World Economic Forum*, November 13, 2023, https://www.weforum.org/agenda/2023/11/generative-ai-holds-potential-disabilities.

15. Donorbox, "The Nonprofit's Guide to AI: How to Use Artificial Intelligence in the Social Sector," *Donorbox*, accessed August 1, 2023, https://donorbox.org/nonprofit-blog/ai-for-nonprofits.

16. Funraise, "27 Best AI Tools for Nonprofits in 2023," *Funraise*, accessed August 1, 2023, https://www.funraise.org/blog/best-ai-tools-for-nonprofits.

17. Whole Whale, "The Nonprofit's Guide to AI in 2023," *Whole Whale*, accessed August 1, 2023, https://www.wholewhale.com/ai.

18. Wild Apricot, "Best Nonprofit Software – Free and Paid Compared and Reviewed," *Wild Apricot*, accessed August 1, 2023, https://www.wildapricot.com/blog/best-nonprofit-software.

CHAPTER 4

Interviews, Outlooks, Testimonials, Quotes

In this chapter, we present insights, perspectives, and real-world examples from leaders in the AI, nonprofit, and business sectors on leveraging artificial intelligence to drive impact and further the missions of nonprofit organizations. Through a series of interviews, quotes, and testimonials, these visionaries share their experiences harnessing the power of AI to boost productivity, gain data-driven insights, revolutionize fundraising, and more. They also discuss ethics, bias, transparency, and trust considerations when implementing AI in the nonprofit context. For many interviews, the author provides a paraphrased recap of key points along with quotes.

The content of the interviews and quotes highlights AI's immense potential to be a catalyst for good when thoughtfully and responsibly deployed by mission-driven organizations. At the same time, it underscores the need for nonprofit leaders to address AI technology's risks and challenges proactively.

Tondi Allen, Co-founder, Urban City Codes
Urban City Codes provides culturally focused community-based learning solutions that empower underrepresented

under-resourced individuals, groups, and businesses to develop and be competitive in a technology-driven economy.

- Recommends Amy Webb's future trends report on AI, Web3, metaverse, bioengineering, robotics, and more. This report provides a futurist perspective on where technology is headed.
- Urban City Codes (UCC) has been using ChatGPT/ GenAI to generate creative fundraising ideas and provide inspiration and structured lists of ideas.
- UCC is also using AI to help create content for workshops and educational programming for their tech students.

Cal Al-Dhubaib, Head of AI and Data Science at Further
FURTHER's team of AI-powered sales assistants collaborates to automate conversations with senior living prospects, helping them find what they're looking for faster.

- AI can amplify and perpetuate biases present in training data, such as gender bias in resume screening, so caution should be used, and outcomes reviewed.
- Reframing the problem AI is trying to solve can help reduce bias and find better solutions (e.g. using AI to identify transportation barriers rather than just predicting no-shows for medical appointments).
- Consistent risk assessment, "red-teaming" (trying to find systems' weaknesses by thinking like attackers), data cards (summaries of data used to train AI including sources and quality), and model cards (how an AI model works, including intended uses and limitations) are important for mitigating unintended harmful consequences of AI.
- AI literacy and training are crucial for nonprofits adopting AI – covering safety, overall digital and AI literacy, and readiness for AI.

Patrick Callihan, CEO, Tech Impact

Tech Impact is a nonprofit and national leader in technology services and training. Their Data Innovation Lab develops talent and works with state agencies and nonprofits to gather, store, and use data for decision-making and solution development.

- They have developed applications that leverage data to identify various issues, such as geographical gaps in healthcare access and tracking outcomes for community revitalization efforts.
- Data can be used to tell stories, articulate challenges around diversity and equity, and inform policies. However, the tools need to be tested for potential bias.
- Over the next 5 to 10 years, data will be increasingly used in the nonprofit sector for decision-making, outcome tracking, proposal writing, and constituent communication.
- Transparency is key to representing data meaningfully. Privacy considerations are also critical when using data and AI.

Allison Fine, President of Every.org and Co-author of *The Smart Nonprofit*

Every.org is a technology platform connecting people and nonprofits through a simple and social giving experience. It's free for nonprofits.

- Allison has spent her career in the nonprofit sector and became interested in the potential of technology in the early 2000s to move power from inside systems to outside groups and individuals.
- AI can potentially take on administrative tasks and free people up to focus on more creative, emotionally engaging work. Leaders who don't understand the tech may just use AI to do more of the same, or "supersize status

quo," versus leveraging time gains for innovation and reducing staff burnout.

♦ Generative AI can be excellent at jumpstarting content development and writing. Machine learning can match people to causes they care about. Advanced AI can help customize donor stories.

♦ AI will change every job – whether or not leaders shape it to benefit workers and clients. Now is the crucial time to shape the future of AI and work.

♦ The nonprofit sector could establish clear policies on data use, privacy, testing for bias, etc., to establish itself as one of AI's most ethical user groups.

Sean Gardner, Forbes Influencer, AI Specialist

Sean is a sought-after nonprofit thought leader currently involved with several book projects and a film project – and gives keynote addresses, presentations, and live TV commentary – on AI and related topics globally.

♦ The UN has embraced AI through its annual AI for Good conference and the creation of an AI Advisory Body.

♦ AI tools are becoming more affordable for nonprofits.

♦ Resources like Coursera, Let's Level Up, UDEMY, and Udacity are valuable for staying updated on AI trends.

♦ It's important to consider diversity, equity, and inclusion when developing AI systems to avoid perpetuating biases, and working with diverse groups of people throughout all steps of creating or implementing AI is key.

Beth Kanter, Nonprofit Innovator, Co-author of *The Smart Nonprofit*

Beth is a trainer, consultant, and nonprofit innovator in digital transformation and workplace well-being, and is recognized by Fast Company and the NTEN Lifetime Achievement Award.

♦ The adoption of AI in the nonprofit sector is still in its early stages, and there is often a tendency to overestimate a technology's short-term impact while underestimating its long-term implications.

◆ As AI frees up time by automating tasks, nonprofit leaders should allow for some "job crafting," where employees have more autonomy to design their roles around their strengths and interests.

◆ Upskilling and reskilling is critical, especially for communities. There are significant initiatives by DataKind, Microsoft, and others focused on workforce development and filling skills gaps.

◆ The shift toward a "skills first" hiring approach, although it's not widely implemented yet, and the necessity of learning AI skills, such as prompt engineering, for everyone to know how to work with AI in their jobs, are discussed.

Cyrus Kazi, CEO, Quantibly.com

Quantibly is the first platform to operationalize impact data collection, analysis, and reporting for the social impact sector.

◆ Quantibly is a data platform that helps nonprofits and NGOs operationalize impact data collection, analysis, and reporting. It automates tasks to save organizations time and currently enables nonprofits to serve 2.8 million people in 82 countries. Nonprofits using it see at least 30% time savings and 20% cost savings. (Disclosure: the author is on Quantibly's advisory board.)

◆ Critical use cases include using AI models to automate data/report generation, grant writing, and impact trend forecasting. They plan to tie United Nations Sustainable Development Goals (SDGs) benchmarking tools into the platform, to better analyze impact.

◆ AI can be used by nonprofits to design services tailored to diverse populations' cultural, religious, language, and other unique needs. Bias in AI models is a concern. Data scientists must minimize selection bias when building for the social impact sector through codes of conduct and ethical standards.

- Emerging AI trends impacting nonprofits include predictive AI to forecast hard-to-quantify social trends and tools to help individuals with impact, such as managing their carbon footprint and promoting responsible consumption.
- Quantibly takes a consent-based approach to data privacy and transparency, believing users own their data. Enforceable global standards are needed for social impact data.

Jason (Jace) A. Martin, Venture Capitalist, President of the Film Council of Greater Columbus

The Columbus International Film + Animation Festival is a Columbus, Ohio, United States, annual film festival designed to encourage and promote film and video in all forms of education and communication. It is the first and oldest film festival in the United States since 1952.

- AI is a useful tool for generating ideas and reconnecting concepts in your mind, but old information may be inaccurate or biased. AI can give confidence by reaffirming previously learned things.
- AI code in cybersecurity may be more easily cracked since it's mass-produced; hackers can easily access it.
- Having enough people in cybersecurity as needs grow due to AI may be challenging, especially with barriers to entry, such as certain cybersecurity jobs that require specific types of military clearance.
- AI-generated film submissions are starting to be included in festivals, signaling a new openness to this subset of films in the space.
- There is concern that the "digital divide" may worsen, with certain groups being left behind if they are not already involved with AI.

Julie Maurer, PhD, Lead Research Manager, Ohio Education Research Center, John Glenn College of Public Affairs at The Ohio State University

The Ohio Education Research Center (OERC) addresses critical education practice and policy issues through a preschool-through-workforce research agenda. The OERC identifies and shares successful practices, responds to the needs of educators and policymakers in Ohio and across the nation, and signals emerging trends.

- AI/ML can potentially introduce bias when generating lists of prospective participants for nonprofit recruitment efforts. This happened on a recent project, leading to the rejection of the AI approach due to inherent disadvantaging risks with certain groups.
- Generative AI provides a path for nonprofits to improve evidence-based decision-making and workflow efficiency and reduce the burden on a constrained workforce as they become more data-driven. This frees up workers to focus on uniquely human capabilities.
- AI is not replacing humans but rather enabling a machine-plus-human approach to work that leverages each other's strengths. This requires trust and adaptability.
- Nonprofits should be courageous in adopting AI or risk being disadvantaged. The benefits span the entire organization. Take advantage of resources to offset costs, but always ask, "Who is being left behind?" In a 2020 study on the future of work, many vulnerable groups were identified as at risk of being left behind by technological disruption, including communities of color, the economically disadvantaged, ex-offenders, immigrants/refugees, and more.
- Providing support systems and removing barriers for disadvantaged workers is key. Nonprofits can apply these insights internally and through their missions.

Craig Newmark, Philanthropist, Founder, Craig Newmark Philanthropies and Craigslist.org
Craig Newmark is best known as the founder of the classifieds ad site craigslist, which showed tens of millions of Americans that the Internet could be reasonably useful and easy to use. Now, he engages in full-time philanthropy, focusing on helping and protecting the people who help and protect our country. That includes cybersecurity, trustworthy journalism, and support for military families and veterans.

- Paid Leave AI is a promising example of using AI for improved customer service to help people access government benefits, which could be expanded to other areas.
- AI-based customer service has significant potential but requires commitment from companies/agencies and ongoing training of AI models by experienced customer service reps. Companies/agencies not prioritizing AI-powered customer service may fall behind.
- The tech industry has been slow to recognize some ethical implications of AI, including potential harm to children. Common Sense Media provides valuable guidance and recommendations for parents and teachers regarding AI and kids' safety.

Leon Wilson, Chief of Digital Innovation and Chief Information Officer at The Cleveland Foundation

- Wilson attended a two-day Microsoft Copilot launch event in Bellevue where they did case studies and demos showcasing how AI is being leveraged using Copilot and saw strong opportunities.
- People are intrigued by AI, but they are still figuring out viable use cases beyond basic productivity enhancements like summarizing meeting notes and drafting documents.

- ◆ Wilson's organization is experimenting with Copilot, giving one license to a person in each department to identify business use cases and get feedback.
- ◆ Wilson sees the potential of using AI to create recommendation engines for things like analyzing grant applications to measure validity for funding based on certain parameters (while still reviewing with a human touch).

Additional Book Contributors (Quotes or Short Interviews):

Jason Feig, Midwest Regional Sales Manager, Khan Academy

Caleb Gardner, Founding Partner: 18 Coffees, Author, Speaker

Melanie McGee, Founder and CEO, We Can Code IT

Rock Christopher Paul, Founder SuccessCENTER.com, Author of *AI Creation Apps*

Devin Thorpe, CEO, The Super Crowd, Author, TV Host, and Speaker at Superpowers for Good

Oxana Vusova, Impact Strategist, Associate Instructor, Columbia University

Lotay Yang, CFP®, Founder BlackCardCircle.com

AI as a Productivity Powerhouse

This section shares quotes from thought leaders expressing how AI can automate tasks and improve productivity and efficiency in nonprofit organizations. Quotes include examples of AI applications in administrative tasks, content creation, and data analysis, highlighting the potential for time savings and increased productivity. From automating routine administrative tasks to enabling smarter decision-making, AI empowers nonprofits to do more with less and focus their human capital on higher-value, mission-oriented work.

AI-powered tools like intelligent chatbots or virtual assistants, robotic process automation (RPA), and machine learning are being leveraged to streamline processes, reduce costs, and ultimately expand impact.

Tondi Allen, Co-founder, Urban City Codes
"ChatGPT is a problem solver for many different things, like when you need a little inspiration . . . maybe with fundraising ideas."

Allison Fine, President of Every.org and Co-author of *The Smart Nonprofit*
"My greatest hope for AI is that it can pick up a lot of [rote or tedious] tasks and free people up [for more creative and people-focused work]. At the same time, my greatest fear is that people in charge of these organizations who don't understand the tech or are driven by fear will use [found time] just to do more of the same."

Cyrus Kazi, CEO, Quantibly.com
"We've been working on an AI model for the nonprofit sector to achieve the following: to automate data and report generation, using the awesome power of AI, and let nonprofits and NGOs write quality grant proposals and impact reports in less than a minute, cutting down this time from an average of four weeks."

Jason (Jace) A. Martin, Venture Capitalist
"Generative AI is a great first-step tool to generate ideas."

Melanie McGee, Founder and CEO, We Can Code IT
"Honestly, if I'm not engaging AI in nearly all aspects of my job, I don't think I'm optimizing my time."

Julie Maurer, PhD, Lead Research Manager, Ohio Education Research Center, John Glenn College of Public Affairs at The Ohio State University

"As nonprofit organizations become increasingly capable of collecting, storing, analyzing, and even sharing data, generative AI provides a path to improving evidence-based decision-making. Moreover, it also improves workflow efficiency and reduces the burden on an often-constrained workforce. The time saved by not having to do certain tasks allows workers to focus on activities that require uniquely human capabilities, such as creativity, critical thinking, and leadership."

Craig Newmark, Philanthropist, Founder, Craig Newmark Philanthropies and Craigslist.org

"The future of good customer service might start with training large language models in what's available already. Then the next step would be committing experienced customer service reps to both helping with customer service and training the language models in anything new that they've just learned, or maybe they're just clarifying what's already there."

Jason Feig, Midwest Regional Sales Manager, Khan Academy

"The things I'm hearing [from educators] are things like, 'Hey, is this going to take my job? How does it impact my work?' You hear a lot of these areas of reflection. And so, we're constantly reassuring that teachers matter, high-quality instruction is [priority] number one [and AI can assist in enabling more time for that piece]."

Oxana Vusova, Impact Strategist, Associate Instructor, Columbia University

"ChatGPT/GenAI is able to help draft a proposal in minutes compared to hours for a human. It really drives home the productivity benefits AI can provide timewise for resource-strapped nonprofits."

Leon Wilson, Chief of Digital Innovation and Chief Information Officer at The Cleveland Foundation

"If you play with AI for any amount of time, the productivity savings are clear at the ground level, including [many use cases like] summarizing meeting minutes, summarizing notes, helping with draft writing for speeches, Word documents, and PowerPoint presentations and synthesizing information from a transcript or report . . . you get all the fundamentals right there."

Data-Driven Insights for Impact

This section shares how AI can be used for data analysis, visualization, and predictive modeling to inform decision-making and improve program outcomes. Quotes focus on examples of AI applications in impact measurement, program evaluation, and predictive analytics, demonstrating the power of data-driven insights for social impact.

These quotes reveal how machine learning and predictive modeling can help organizations better understand their stakeholders, identify trends and opportunities, optimize programs and interventions, and make more informed decisions.

The use cases and best practices illustrate the power of AI-driven insights to help nonprofits achieve better outcomes, from enhancing donor segmentation for targeted fundraising appeals to predicting beneficiary needs for more personalized service delivery.

Cyrus Kazi, CEO, Quantibly.com

"Use AI to forecast or predict impact trends within the organization vis-à-vis the macro benchmarks, such as sustainable development goals (SDGs). For example, a nonprofit . . . can use [Quantibly] to forecast if they are on track to meeting their impact goals and compare their achievements to other changemakers contributing to a specific SDG."

Patrick Callihan, CEO, Tech Impact

"Data can be used to tell a story. What is the number of people in tech? How many of those are from underrepresented communities?

It can help to articulate the challenges in a community, among a group of individuals, or show a lack of diversity or equity. Data can help unlock those stories. It is difficult to argue with data that is factual."

Leon Wilson, Chief of Digital Innovation and Chief Information Officer at The Cleveland Foundation
"We are definitely trying to push it a little bit more to try to leverage AI to say, can we now use it to create a pseudo recommendation engine that if we add numerous good examples of grants, which ones should we consider funding based on these parameters [under supervision]."

Revolutionizing Fundraising and Grant Development
Development professionals and AI experts here discuss how artificial intelligence transforms nonprofit fundraising, grant seeking, and development processes. Discover how forward-thinking organizations use machine learning algorithms to identify and prioritize the most promising donor and grant identification prospects, tailor solicitation strategies, and personalize outreach, grant writing, and reporting, potentially increasing funding and resource acquisition.

The interviews and insights shared paint an exciting picture of AI's potential to help nonprofits raise more money more efficiently from a wider support base to fuel their missions. At the same time, they raise important questions about the responsible and ethical use of AI in fundraising that every nonprofit leader must grapple with.

Allison Fine, President of Every.org and Co-author of *The Smart Nonprofit*
"Machine learning can pair people up with causes. You could put in criteria like the issue area you care about and your zip code and find smaller organizations you might not have found before. More advanced AI can help nonprofits customize stories for individual donors, based on what you've liked before, what your preferences are, what you've clicked on.

That has some huge benefits. Those are the areas that we're exploring at Every.org."

Cyrus Kazi, CEO, Quantibly.com
"The applications of AI in the nonprofit sector are limitless, in my opinion. One of the top ways nonprofits can use AI is to design products and services that can address the needs of diverse populations, accounting for their cultural, religious, and language needs."

Oxana Vusova, Impact Strategist, Associate Instructor, Columbia University
"AI can be used for donor prospecting, diversifying donor portfolios, and tailoring messaging to different audiences to illustrate multiple powerful applications."

Addressing Bias and Ethical Concerns
This section explores the critical issues of bias and ethics, the critical considerations surrounding bias in AI algorithms, and the need for ethical development and implementation by nonprofits. Through thought-provoking interviews with ethicists, activists, and nonprofit executives, we explore the risks and pitfalls of relying on AI systems that may perpetuate or amplify societal biases and inequities and how organizations can mitigate them.

Nonprofits can proactively audit their AI implementations for bias, establishing ethical guidelines and oversight mechanisms while investing in diversity and inclusion to create AI that reflects their values. The perspectives shared underscore the urgent moral imperative for nonprofits to ensure their use of this technology promotes rather than undermines equity and the need for ongoing monitoring and evaluation to ensure equitable outcomes.

Cal Al-Dhubaib, Head of AI and Data Science at Further
"If the examples [used to train AI] reflect negative biases, AI will learn to perpetuate these examples. Let's say you're building an

AI application to screen resumes and the majority of qualified candidates, historically, have been male. It's plausible to assume that the model may pick up on attributes in the resumes that skew male."

"In many cases, it's not really a data problem. It's how you frame the problem you're trying to solve. A recent example I loved was a children's hospital looking to minimize no-show rates . . . Instead of using AI to predict no-show rates and double booking, one could redesign the problem to identify when nominal interventions, like an Uber credit, are more likely to get a patient to the appointment."

Patrick Callihan, CEO, Tech Impact

"Be wary of the tools that you're using. They are programmed by individuals; do they have inherent bias? Many recruiting tools have been shown to have bias built in. Test for bias; are the tools really giving you the results you intend? Are they leaving some people behind based on their background or even their name or education level? There are so many pitfalls here that this type of technology needs to be approached to look at any unintended consequences."

Allison Fine, President of Every.org and Co-author of *The Smart Nonprofit*

"I really think that in the nonprofit sector, we could put our flag in the ground as the most ethical users of AI. We could be out front on this, but we'd have to be doing this right now by saying all of our organizations are going to have clear policies on data use and privacy, and making sure that AI is at least testing for bias.

"We could have a set of principles that we follow, about making sure that we have representational teams doing the hard work on the bias piece . . . now's the moment. If we do, I think we can bring great people into the sector and keep great people in the sector. If we can be real leaders on this, I think it will be a huge attraction for folks who care about these issues.

"Whether AI is to benefit the worker and the ultimate client is a leadership issue, not a technology issue. So much of this comes back to what our leaders will choose to do in the future with AI to improve work and workers."

Sean Gardner, Forbes Influencer, AI Specialist

"I would urge nonprofits to carefully consider if their AI system was created with recommendations from a diverse and vibrant group of people. This is important because a recent investigation by Bloomberg found that OpenAI's ChatGPT showed racial bias when screening resumes for jobs. So yes, integrate DEI [diversity, equity, and inclusion] in your AI design. You don't want any of your inclusive initiatives to end up perpetuating bias."

Cyrus Kazi, CEO, Quantibly.com

"An AI model is as good as the developers that build them. As such, data scientists need to minimize their selection bias when building for the social impact sector. In order to build AI models to minimize biases, it's imperative that certain codes of conduct and ethical standards are put forth and that these values are reflected in the data selection and training models."

Jace Martin, Venture Capitalist

"AI can reconnect ideas on the periphery of your brain you forgot you knew. However, it could be problematic simultaneously because if you remembered things from years ago, you may not know if this information might be biased or outdated.

"The 'digital divide' [access to technology devices and connectivity that supports AI] may get greater, leaving people behind with specific effects on certain groups of [underserved] people; in other words, if you are not already in the [AI and technology] game . . . you can get left behind."

Julie Maurer, PhD, Lead Research Manager, Ohio Education Research Center, John Glenn College of Public Affairs at The Ohio State University
"Concerns were expressed by several members of the team that the algorithms (ML) deployed to generate the lists from a very large dataset could be biased against certain groups. At the center of the expressed concerns was the question of bias being introduced into the process of creating 'ideal participant' profiles based on factors such as geography, age, driver's license status, education attainment, and other individual characteristics."

Craig Newmark, Philanthropist, Founder, Craig Newmark Philanthropies and Craigslist.org
"[Many] technologists . . . are slow to recognize the ethical implications of new technologies. This has been very true of the entire range of large language model work . . . [but also,] there's a lot of good work addressing issues of bias in AI."

Oxana Vusova, Impact Strategist, Associate Instructor, Columbia University
"AI augments rather than replacing humans . . . this is an impor tant [idea] that pushes back against fears of job losses. It positions AI as a tool to enhance nonprofit work."

Transparency and Building Trust

Nonprofit and AI leaders share their hard-won insights as follows on the importance of transparency and data privacy in building stakeholder trust and confidence in AI-powered solutions. Their organizations are taking new approaches to clearly communicate how AI is being used, the safeguards in place, and the results achieved, both internally and externally.

From establishing AI governance frameworks to engaging in public education and dialogue, the strategies and lessons offer a new paradigm of openness and accountability around AI in the nonprofit sector. Emphasis should be placed on the need for clear communication with stakeholders about how AI is being used, the importance of data security and privacy protocols, and the role of transparency in building trust with donors, beneficiaries, and the wider community.

Patrick Callihan, CEO, Tech Impact

"Transparency is at the center of our work. One of the greatest benefits of data and AI is transparency. This is particularly true in our work with government agencies and nonprofits. To be able to represent data factually and visually is what allows for transparency. Constituents can easily access and see information in a way that is meaningful to them."

Cal Al-Dhubaib, Head of AI and Data Science at Further

"Red-teaming and consistent risk assessment processes are the best defenses against unintended consequences. The results are communicated in tools known as 'data cards' and 'model cards'. Even if you're not building these AI tools, I encourage you to ask your vendors for their data and model cards. If these assets aren't available or can't be readily produced, that's a big red flag."

Cyrus Kazi, CEO, Quantibly.com

"Our approach to nonprofit data privacy and transparency is borrowed from the Trust Framework and Code of Conduct set by the CARIN Alliance, a multisector group of healthcare stakeholders that advocate for consumer control of their data. We believe that our end-users are the owners of their data, and they have the right to access their information at any time."

A Call to Action: Embracing the AI Future

In this culminating section, leaders issue a passionate call to action for the nonprofit sector to proactively embrace the

AI revolution. They make the case for why nonprofits cannot afford to sit on the sidelines as this technology reshapes our world, and how those that do so risk losing relevance and impact.

At the same time, they challenge nonprofits to lead the way in shaping an AI future that puts people and purpose first and leverages this powerful tool to create a more just, equitable, and sustainable society. Their insights and provocations will leave you energized and empowered to seize the opportunities of AI with courage and conviction, while mitigating the risks with care and foresight.

Cal Al-Dhubaib, Head of AI and Data Science at Further
"You need three forms of AI training for your workforce – safety, literacy, and readiness:

1. Safety prepares your workforce to recognize increasingly sophisticated AI-generated phishing attacks, scams, and fake information.
2. Literacy helps your workforce understand what to expect of AI – how harmful biases might occur, when it may be safe to trust the results of an AI solution, and what questions to ask of vendors to sort hype from reality.
3. Readiness is empowering individuals with skills to confidently use AI tools to perform their work – this will be specialized by role and specific tool."

Patrick Callihan, CEO, Tech Impact
"Like any disruptive technology, there are many upsides. There are also pitfalls. Think about the ways in which you will consider using the technology. Build a plan that outlines the various use cases for your organization. Rank them by the potential ROI [return on investment] of the technology adoption. Where will the organization get the most return for the lowest investment, etc. It is imperative that the organization continue to research AI and the use of AI in nonprofits."

Allison Fine, President of Every.org and Co-author of *The Smart Nonprofit*

"[If the nonprofit sector waits to see how things change with AI] it will have happened already. Right now . . . there's a sliver of an opportunity to shape work and workers for the next generation."

Sean Gardner, Forbes Influencer, AI Specialist

"I would urge nonprofits to carefully [ensure] that their AI system was created with recommendations from a diverse and vibrant group of people."

Beth Kanter, Nonprofit Innovator, Co-author of *The Smart Nonprofit*

"The stuff that [AI] can't do, which is uniquely human, like interacting, interpersonal skills, communication, storytelling, creativity [will be increasingly important for people]. Although . . . some of the software is pretty good at brainstorming, the human relationship [pieces], traditionally called soft skills, become more valued, [underscoring] the ongoing importance of human skills and the need for nonprofit leaders to invest in staff development."

Cyrus Kazi, CEO, Quantibly.com

"Predictive AI is an emerging trend in the nonprofit sector . . . Powerful and generative AI models would be capable of understanding and mathematically forecasting social trends that are often not quantifiable or even well-defined."

Julie Maurer, PhD, Lead Research Manager, Ohio Education Research Center, John Glenn College of Public Affairs at The Ohio State University

"Be courageous and deploy your change management capabilities. The nonprofit sector is evolving quickly and choosing not to adopt AI solutions will increasingly disadvantage your organization in ways that may not be immediately obvious. The benefits of adopting new technologies are far-reaching and span across your entire organization – from strategic planning to customer service, fundraising, and all other areas of the operation.

"Across groups, a key strategy identified for strengthening the future workforce is to provide support systems and access to opportunities for those who are disadvantaged and lack work-based benefits. This includes removing barriers created by the lack of affordable and convenient transportation, childcare, housing, healthcare, food, and other basic needs. Not only can nonprofit organizations benefit from applying these insights to managing their own teams, but their missions often aim to provide these critical support services for the most vulnerable workers."

Craig Newmark, Philanthropist, Founder, Craig Newmark Philanthropies and Craigslist.org
"Fortunately, Common Sense Media has been addressing these issues and discussing related matters with parents and teachers for a long time. Their recommendations regarding TV and movies are seriously helpful, and very effective. Now, they're offering guardrails and recommending specific AI sites for kids. The work being done by Common Sense Media is a really big deal for the entire AI industry."

Summary
The voices of these experts paint a vivid picture of the evolving AI landscape in the nonprofit sector. While challenges and ethical considerations remain, the potential for AI to empower nonprofits and accelerate positive change is undeniable. By embracing a spirit of innovation, collaboration, and responsible implementation, nonprofits can harness the power of AI to create a more just, equitable, and impactful future.

CHAPTER 5

Case Studies

Current Case Studies of AI Implementation for Core Nonprofit Functions Like Fundraising, Grants, Marketing, and Initiative Event Optimization

Empowering Your Nonprofit with AI: Real-World Case Studies

A transformative era is here for nonprofits. In the relentless pursuit of a more just and sustainable world, nonprofit organizations stand at the forefront of possibilities. Artificial Intelligence (AI) emerges as a powerful tool, unlocking unprecedented efficiency and efficacy that can lead to more social impact.

In this chapter, we peer into the real-world experiences of fellow pioneers who have embraced AI integration. A curated selection of case studies will help us explore how these organizations have successfully leveraged AI technologies to enhance core functions like research analysis, fundraising, grant development, communications outreach, marketing, and event planning.

Keep in mind that the value of human touch when leveraging AI is becoming even more valuable, and AI should not typically be seen as "replacing" people as much as it can be seen to help offload certain tasks to free up time or augment skills.

As Beth Kanter, nonprofit innovator and co-author of the book, *The Smart Nonprofit*, notes:

> Interacting, interpersonal skills, communication, storytelling, creativity . . . some of the software is pretty good at brainstorming, but the human relationship side, what's traditionally called soft skills, has to become more valued.

LEARNING FROM LEADERS

These narratives offer invaluable insights and inspiration, showcasing AI's tangible benefits and untapped potential in the nonprofit sector. Each case study provides a holistic understanding of AI implementation's strategies and challenges, focusing on outcomes demonstrating how AI can inform decision-making and amplify social impact.

ADAPTING AND APPLYING

As you immerse yourself in these stories, consider how the lessons learned and best practices shared can be adapted and applied to your organization's unique context. Pay close attention to key success factors such as leadership buy-in, data readiness, stakeholder engagement, and ethical considerations, which are crucial for effective AI deployment in the nonprofit realm.

CHARTING YOUR COURSE

Whether your organization seeks to leverage AI for program planning, fundraising, grant development, marketing, or community-driven innovation, these case studies offer practical guidance and tangible evidence of its transformative power. By learning from the experiences of other nonprofits, you can make informed decisions and chart a course toward successful

AI adoption tailored to your organization's needs, all while circumventing common pitfalls.

REMEMBER

AI is not a one-size-fits-all solution. Each nonprofit's journey will be uniquely shaped by its mission. Additionally, the resources a nonprofit has available and the unique stakeholders' needs are important factors. Treat these case studies as a jumping-off point for ideation and inspiration, but be prepared to adapt and innovate as you explore the possibilities of AI for your organization.

AMPLIFYING YOUR IMPACT

The ultimate goal is to amplify your impact and better serve the communities you support. With the right approach, mindset, commitment to learning, and strategy that aligns with goals, AI can empower your nonprofit to achieve unprecedented levels of social change. Let these case studies guide you as you navigate the exciting frontier of AI, co-creating a future where technology and human ingenuity converge to drive positive, lasting impact.

Case Study Examples

AMERICAN CANCER SOCIETY

The American Cancer Society has leveraged AI to hyper-personalize its digital fundraising campaigns. By feeding historical donor data, supporter profiles, and real-time engagement signals into machine learning algorithms, the organization developed predictive models that could identify the specific messaging, channels, and timing most likely to resonate with each prospective giver. This increased donation revenue to 117% higher than its benchmark, plus donor engagement rose to nearly 70% during the campaign.[1]

CRISIS TEXT LINE

By using AI to analyze 2.8 million conversations to uncover who is most at risk during a spike in demand, Crisis Text Line has been able to help direct support where it is needed most. Artificial intelligence helped them adjust their thresholds of risk more accurately and reduce the wait time of the highest-risk users from 25 minutes to around 3 minutes.[2]

These are just two examples of the transformative ways nonprofits are harnessing AI across their core functions. From streamlining grant writing to optimizing program delivery, the applications of AI technology continue to evolve. As the nonprofit sector grapples with intensifying challenges, the strategic embrace of AI will be increasingly essential in driving sustainable operations.

Case Study – Programs and Initiative Planning

Nonprofits often face the challenge of effectively allocating limited resources to maximize their impact. AI offers a powerful solution by providing data-driven insights that inform program planning and initiative deployment. These insights can help nonprofits identify trends and patterns and adapt their programs to changing circumstances.

Program and initiative planning and measurement can be enhanced by leveraging AI. One way to do this is to use AI "to forecast or predict impact trends within the organization vis-à-vis macro benchmarks, such as the United Nations Sustainable Development Goals (SDGs). For example, a nonprofit working [within a specific SDG] can use AI to forecast if they are on track to meeting their impact goals and compare their achievements to other changemakers contributing to a specific sustainable development goal," explains Cyrus Kazi, CEO of social impact measurement platform Quantibly (author is on the board of advisors). In this way, performance can be benchmarked to see if any changes might be helpful.

In these case studies, we will explore how nonprofits can leverage AI technologies to enhance their programs and initiatives within planning, implementation, and evaluation. By harnessing the power of data analytics, predictive modeling, and other AI tools, nonprofits can gain valuable insights and a deeper understanding of the needs and preferences of target communities. AI can also help optimize resource allocation and improve the effectiveness and impact of interventions, and help nonprofits make data-driven decisions. Identifying trends and patterns can help provide ideas for how to best adapt their programs to changing circumstances.

The AI model's ability to learn and adapt is particularly noteworthy. As new challenges emerge or priorities shift, the system dynamically adjusts its analysis, providing up-to-date and actionable guidance. This adaptive planning is crucial for navigating the complexities of various nonprofit sectors in rapidly changing times.

For instance, a literacy nonprofit utilizes AI to personalize tutoring programs. By analyzing student data, the AI model recommends the most effective curriculum pathways and automatically adjusts based on individual progress, leading to improved learning outcomes. Similarly, a homeless services group leverages AI to optimize volunteer scheduling, intake interviews, and critical appointments, enhancing operational efficiency and better meeting individual needs.

From using machine learning algorithms to predict beneficiary outcomes to employing natural language processing to analyze feedback and sentiment, these case studies will showcase the wide-ranging applications of AI in program planning and management, focusing on diverse organizations and social justice causes.

Here are case studies of nonprofit organizations with a focus on using AI for operations, planning, and administrative tasks:

- ♦ **Increase Civic Engagement: NAACP**
  The NAACP partnered with AI company Evelynn to develop an AI virtual assistant to provide voting information

and resources to African American communities before the 2022 midterm elections.[3]

♦ **Crisis Counseling: The Trevor Project**

The Trevor Project implemented an AI-powered crisis counseling platform called "AI+Human" to support LGBTQ youth. It combines conversational AI with human counselors.[4]

♦ **Resource Planning: UN Refugee Agency (UNHCR)**

The United Nations High Commissioner for Refugees (UNHCR) has leveraged machine learning for demand forecasting and optimizing distribution of resources like shelters and winterization kits for refugee camps.[5]

♦ **Career Readiness: National Urban League**

The Urban League used IBM Watson AI to create a virtual career assistant providing personalized career coaching, mentoring, and skill development resources.[6]

♦ **Language Translation: Translators without Borders**

This nonprofit leveraged AI translation models and localization tools to provide vital information in multiple languages during humanitarian crises.[7]

♦ **Data Analysis: Compassion International**

Compassion International identifies patterns to improve their child sponsorship programs. They leverage AI to predict which children are most at risk and target interventions accordingly.[8]

♦ **Satellite Imagery Analysis: The Audubon Society**

Identifying important bird habitats for conservation efforts using satellite imagery helps the Audubon Society improve its impact by more effectively planning and prioritizing its initiatives.[9]

♦ **Simplify Paid Leave Application: Paid Leave AI**

Paid Leave AI is a service that helps New Yorkers understand and claim their paid family leave benefits. It simplifies the complicated process of applying for paid family leave, acting as a personal navigator to guide users through policies and paperwork. Ultimately, it provides a clear, emailed action plan to complete and submit their claim.[10]

While still emerging, these examples showcase how nonprofits strategically utilize AI to enhance program delivery, optimize resources, personalize services, and drive impact in diverse communities worldwide, leveraging AI for programs and initiatives.

Case Study – Funding Campaigns

Fundraising is critical for all nonprofit organizations. Artificial Intelligence technologies offer powerful tools to optimize and streamline the fundraising process. In these case studies, we will examine how nonprofits can use AI to analyze donor data, predict giving behavior, personalize outreach and engagement strategies, and otherwise harness the power of data to create actionable insights.

By leveraging machine learning algorithms trained on historical donation data and donor profiles, as well as market and giving trends, organizations can develop predictive models to identify promising prospective donors and recommend optimal appeal strategies. The results can be remarkable, with a significant increase in new donor acquisition and a boost in recurring donations after implementing an AI-powered fundraising system.

AI's impact extends beyond large organizations. AI-powered chatbots can answer common donor questions, freeing staff for more complex interactions. Nonprofits can use AI to personalize donation appeals, customizing messages, timing, and channels based on past supporter data, resulting in increased response rates and lower acquisition costs.

From chatbots providing personalized donor experiences to predictive models forecasting donation trends, these case studies will highlight how AI can help nonprofits secure the resources they need to advance their missions. These examples demonstrate how AI empowers nonprofits to improve fundraising performance, engagement, and donation conversion rates through predictive modeling, conversational AI, audience optimization, and other innovative capabilities.

Here are case studies of nonprofit organizations that leverage AI for funding campaigns and fundraising initiatives:

- **Increase Fundraising Engagement: Good360.org**
  Nonprofits can leverage AI tools to analyze donor data, segmenting supporters based on their giving patterns, interests, and demographics. This enables organizations to tailor personalized fundraising appeals and optimize their campaigns for maximum impact.[11]
- **Enhance Visitor Engagement: The World Wildlife Fund (WWF)**
  WWF is one of the many nonprofits leveraging AI-powered chatbots to enhance visitor engagement on their website. These chatbots are designed to interact with users, provide information, answer questions, and streamline the donation process.[12]
- **Member Engagement: NAACP**
  The NAACP implemented an AI virtual assistant to engage members, provide information about initiatives, solicit feedback, and process donations.[13]
- **Image Recognition: National Geographic Society**
  AI-powered image recognition helps organizations catalog their media assets. The technology allows nonprofits to easily search and retrieve images for use in fundraising campaigns and other outreach efforts, making the appeals more relevant and compelling while reducing staff time spent searching for images.[14]
- **Fundraising Support: Dataro**
  Dataro's analytics and propensity modeling software for charities uses machine learning technology to generate predictions about how donors are likely to behave, gleaning new insights from your fundraising data.[15]

While still emerging, these examples show how nonprofits leverage AI capabilities like predictive modeling, conversational AI, audience optimization, and more to improve fundraising performance and increase engagement and donation conversion rates.

Case Study – Grant Development

Securing grants is vital but often time-consuming and competitive for many nonprofits. In these case studies, we will explore how AI technologies can assist nonprofits in identifying relevant grant opportunities and crafting compelling proposals, which can improve their chances of success.

AI tools can help analyze grant databases, identify key trends and priorities, and match nonprofit programs with funder interests, streamlining the grant research and application process for organizations. Additionally, AI-powered writing assistants can help nonprofits draft clear, persuasive, and well-structured proposals, saving time and improving the quality of their submissions. Through practical examples and insights, these case studies will demonstrate the potential of AI to revolutionize the grant development process for nonprofits.

Here are case studies of nonprofit organizations leveraging AI for grant development processes:

- ◆ **Grant Relationship Management: The Rockefeller Foundation**

    The Rockefeller Foundation's AI chatbot called "Rox" provides grant applicants and recipients with information, answers to FAQs, and status updates throughout the grantmaking process.[16]

- ◆ **Racial Wealth Equity through Investment: DataKind**

    By utilizing insights created during the development of the Racial Wealth Equity Database and with support from Google.org and DataKind, Black Wealth Data Center (BWDC) created a tool designed to facilitate access to funding for Black entrepreneurs.[17]

◆ **Connecting Nonprofits, Donors, and Companies: GlobalGiving**

GlobalGiving is a nonprofit that connects nonprofits, donors, and companies globally. They help nonprofits access funding, tools, training, and support to serve their communities. AI helps them automate reporting to increase transparency and accountability and track and analyze outcomes of funded projects.[18]

While direct AI grant writing is still in its early stages, several organizations and platforms are exploring its potential to benefit nonprofits, as discussed in the following sections. Additionally, most generative AI tools like GPT, Claude, Gemini, and similar offer excellent drafting, summarizing, paraphrasing, and other generally useful writing skills that can make grant writing easier.

Grants.gov and AI: The central hub for federal grant opportunities is exploring AI to enhance user experience and streamline the application process. This could potentially include tools to assist with crafting grant proposals in the future.

Resources and Advocacy: Nonprofit Tech for Good: This organization provides resources and promotes the effective use of technology in the nonprofit sector, including discussions on AI's potential for grant writing (nptechforgood.com).

Data and Insights: Candid (formerly Foundation Center and GuideStar): Candid utilizes machine learning and natural language processing to analyze grant data, offering valuable insights that can inform and improve grant applications (candid.org).

Here is a list of other top tools and companies that assist nonprofit organizations with writing, research, searching, finding, or developing grants utilizing AI tools or systems:

- Grantable[19]
- Fundwriter.ai[20]
- Granted AI[21]
- Grantboost[22]
- Instrumentl[23]
- GrantHub[24]
- GrantWatch[25]
- GrantStation[26]
- FoundationSearch[27]
- Grant Gopher[28]
- GrantForward[29]
- Submittable[30]
- Fluxx Grantmaker[31]
- Altum ProposalCentral[32]
- Optimy[33]
- SmartSimple Cloud Grants[34]

These organizations offer various AI-powered tools and services to help nonprofits streamline their grant research, writing, and management processes, ultimately helping them secure more funding to support their missions. The future looks to hold even more ways AI can help streamline grant processes, including application screening, relationship management, grant exploration and writing assistance, and reducing administrative burdens.

Case Study – Nonprofit Marketing and Communications

Effective marketing and communications are essential for nonprofits to raise awareness, engage stakeholders, and mobilize support for their causes in tailored ways. From using machine learning algorithms to segment audiences and personalize messaging to employing predictive analytics to forecast event attendance and resource needs, AI offers a range of powerful tools to enhance nonprofit marketing and event planning. Real-world examples like the following will showcase how nonprofits can leverage AI to create targeted campaigns, improve event experiences, and maximize the impact of their outreach efforts.

Here are case studies of nonprofit organizations leveraging AI for marketing, outreach, and event optimization:

- **Virtual Event Assistants: UNICEF**

  For their virtual events during COVID-19, UNICEF deployed AI Chatbots to digitally register attendees, provide information, and engage audiences. UNICEF regularly uses and researches chatbots for multiple other use cases as well.[35]

- **Overcome Language Barriers: The Children's Society**

  This UK children's charity employed Microsoft Translator's live feature to overcome language barriers when working with young migrants, refugees, and victims of trafficking seeking asylum. By leveraging this AI-powered, in-person translation tool, which utilizes machine learning and neural networks to provide realistic, human-sounding translations, the charity was able to communicate more effectively with its beneficiaries while maintaining a higher level of privacy and trust.[36]

- **Social Listening and Engagement: The Lupus Foundation**

  This health nonprofit leverages AI social listening tools to better understand discussions of lupus, identify influencers, and inform content strategy.[37]

- **Online Hate Speech Monitoring: Anti-Defamation League**

  The ADL partnered with Sporton to develop an AI model to detect hate speech across social platforms for awareness campaigns and policy advocacy.[38]

- **Boosting Membership: Girl Scouts of America**

  The organization used artificial intelligence in a Google search campaign, resulting in a 40% reduction in its membership acquisition costs.[39]

- **Supporter Predictions: Parkinson's UK**

   Partnering with Dataro, this organization used AI-driven supporter predictions to refine an appeal that translated into a potential revenue increase of 23% when focusing on donors identified through machine learning. The AI predictions resulted in over 2,800 individual gifts (versus around 2,500 for the traditional approach) with a smaller list of potential donors.[40]

- **Audience Optimization: American Hospital Association**

   Redefining audience targeting with AI and predictive analytics can help hospitals and healthcare nonprofits focus marketing efforts on potential patients or clients who are most likely to engage in conversations, minimizing marketing waste.[41]

- **Video Creation: The Arizona State Employees Charitable Campaign**

   The Arizona State Employees Charitable Campaign raised awareness for their cause and charities through a video fair. AI has made video creation more efficient and cost-effective for nonprofits, allowing them to engage audiences through video storytelling quickly and affordably.[42]

While still emerging, these examples showcase how nonprofits are leveraging AI's analytical, generative, and interactive capabilities to enhance marketing ROI, create resonant digital campaigns, optimize outreach and events, and drive mission awareness.

Case Study – Collaborative AI Development

Leaders in the nonprofit sector understand the immense potential of technology to drive meaningful change. These case studies explore how collaborative AI development and open-source initiatives can empower organizations to achieve profound impact.

Participation in collaborative AI groups and communities allows organizations to tap into the collective knowledge and expertise of developers, researchers, and domain experts from around the globe. From building custom AI-powered solutions to contributing to shared datasets and models, these collaborative efforts can open new avenues for innovation and social impact.

Cloud-based platforms and capacity-building initiatives enable nonprofits to leverage AI specialists' expertise without requiring extensive in-house technical resources. By tapping into these collaborative ecosystems, you can unlock AI's transformative potential regardless of organizational size or technical capabilities.

While ethical AI development requires diligent consideration, the benefits of these collaborative approaches are clear. By working together, nonprofits can democratize access to AI technologies, accelerate social impact, and drive positive change in their communities.

Here are case studies of nonprofit organizations collaborating on AI development, open-source datasets, and exploring the use of AI technologies:

- **Collaborative AI Development: The Future Society**
  The Future Society partnered with AI companies like Anthropic to develop open-source AI models and tools for social impact use cases.[43]
- **Open Data for AI and Nonprofit Collaborations: DataKind**
  DataKind facilitates collaborations between data scientists and nonprofit domain experts to create open data repositories and AI/ML models for social good.[44]
- **Machine Learning Charity Initiatives: AWS**
  Amazon partnered with groups like the American Red Cross and Path to leverage AWS AI services for social impact projects.[45]

- **Nonprofit Data Sharing and Model Collaboration: AI4Giving**

  AI4Giving is building an open data-sharing platform and co-development of AI models across participating nonprofits like United Way.[46]
- **Funding Ethical AI for Underserved Communities: Lacuna Fund**

  Lacuna provides grants for developing open AI technologies centered around underserved and marginalized communities.[47]
- **AI Capacity Building for Grassroots Nonprofits: Data.org**

  Data.org partners with community nonprofits to provide AI skills training, resources, and collaborative model development opportunities.[48]

While ethical AI development requires care, these examples showcase nonprofits coming together through consortium, open data sharing, participatory approaches, cloud, and capacity building to explore AI's potential for social good collaboratively.

Case Study – Community-Driven AI Innovation

Here we will explore how nonprofits can harness community-driven AI innovation to address complex social challenges and drive positive impact. By engaging diverse stakeholders like beneficiaries/end users, volunteers, and domain experts, nonprofits can co-create AI solutions that are more inclusive, responsive, and impactful.

Community-driven AI innovation involves a participatory approach, where the community is actively involved in all steps in the process, from ideation and design development and deployment. This approach ensures that AI solutions are grounded in the real needs, experiences, and insights of the people they aim to serve. Being mindfully inclusive of different ideas, lived experiences, perspectives, and insights throughout the process leads to more relevant, effective, and sustainable outcomes. By doing this, nonprofits can create inclusive spaces for collaboration, foster a culture of experimentation and learning, and build trust and transparency with stakeholders throughout the AI development process.

This type of comprehensive collaboration allows nonprofits to uncover new ideas, challenge assumptions, and generate innovative AI solutions that may not have been possible through traditional, top-down approaches.

As you explore examples, consider how your own nonprofit can embrace a more participatory and inclusive approach to AI innovation. Reflect on the unique strengths and experiences your community can bring to the table and how you can create meaningful opportunities for collaboration and co-creation. Remember, community-driven AI innovation is not just about developing better technology; it's about empowering people, building resilience, and fostering a sense of ownership and shared responsibility for the solutions that shape our world. By putting the community at the center of your AI efforts, you can unlock the full potential AI technology to drive social good and create a more equitable and sustainable future for all.

Here are case studies of nonprofit organizations utilizing community-driven approaches and grassroots innovations with AI:

- **Community Data Governance Models: Allied Media Projects**

  Allied Media builds community data trusts and governance frameworks for ethical AI development representing marginalized voices.[49]

- **Indigenous AI Application: Digital Democracy**

  This nonprofit partners with indigenous communities to apply technologies like AI to meet environmental mapping and monitoring needs.[50]

- **Community AI Advisory Councils: The Greenlining Institute**

  Greenlining partners with companies like Sutter Health to establish community councils advising on the ethical use of AI.[51]

- **AI for Cardiovascular Research: American Heart Association**

  AI-based tools have the potential to transform cardiovascular care in numerous areas, from diagnosis and disease classification to treatment selection and clinical decision support.[52]

- **Fighting X (Formerly Twitter) Trolls: Amnesty International**

  Thousands of digital activists are helping us build an algorithm that automatically detects online abuse.[53]

- **"Nutrition" Labels for AI to Protect Children: Common Sense Media**

  Common Sense Media is committed to understanding and addressing the impact of AI on children. As AI rapidly advances and integrates into our lives, Common Sense aims to provide clarity, trust, and understanding through initiatives such as AI product ratings and reviews, literacy curricula, and original research. These efforts are guided by eight principles ensuring children's needs are prioritized in an AI-driven future. Their AI reviews provide "nutrition" labels for AI.[54]

These examples showcase nonprofits putting community voices at the forefront by educating and advising, as well as using participatory design, processes, and governance AI models and applications centered around the unique needs of diverse populations.

Ways AI Case Studies Suggest Benefits to Nonprofits

In this chapter, we explored a series of case studies that showcase how innovative nonprofits have leveraged AI to amplify their impact and address complex social challenges.

These case studies offer a wealth of insights and practical strategies that can inspire and guide your own AI adoption journey. By learning from the successes, challenges, and innovations of your peers, you can gain a deeper understanding of how to harness the power of AI to enhance your organization's capabilities and achieve your mission with greater efficiency and impact.

HERE IS A SUMMARY OF HOW AI CAN BENEFIT NONPROFITS

Enhanced Decision-Making
AI-powered data analysis and predictive modeling have empowered nonprofit leaders to make more informed, evidence-based decisions, optimizing resource allocation and strategic planning.

Intelligent Automation
AI can streamline administrative tasks, freeing up valuable staff time and resources for mission-driven initiatives while improving operational efficiency and reducing costs.

Optimized Fundraising
Organizations that have leveraged AI to identify promising prospective donors, personalize outreach, and optimize fundraising campaigns have seen increased donor acquisition, retention, and revenue.

Data-Driven Program Planning
AI's ability to analyze vast datasets can help nonprofits pinpoint critical areas for program initiatives, allocate resources more effectively, and maximize their social impact.

Enhanced Marketing and Events
Many case studies showcase how AI can help nonprofits better understand and engage their target audiences. AI can also personalize marketing content and optimize event strategies, resulting in greater reach, participation, and community involvement.

Personalized Experiences
AI can tailor interactions with donors, volunteers, and beneficiaries based on individual needs and preferences, fostering deeper engagement and stronger relationships.

Predictive Insights
AI-powered analytics can identify potential challenges and opportunities, enabling nonprofits to address issues and make more informed strategic decisions proactively.

Collaborative AI Development
Nonprofits that have embraced open-source AI initiatives and participatory approaches have democratized access to cutting-edge technologies and driven innovation through collective intelligence and shared resources.

Each nonprofit's AI journey will be unique, shaped by specific needs, resources, and organizational culture. Strategies and solutions that work for one organization may require adaptation to suit another. However, by drawing inspiration from these innovative examples and applying the lessons learned, you can confidently navigate your AI transformation and accelerate the positive impact your organization delivers to the communities you serve.

AI's true power – regardless of the specific tools used – lies in its potential to amplify your mission, empower your teams, and drive meaningful change.

Notes
1. "How Nonprofits Use AI to Find and Keep Good Donors," *SAP Insights*, 2023, https://www.sap.com/insights/viewpoints/how-nonprofits-use-ai-to-find-and-keep-good-donors.html.
2. "What We Learned from Training a Machine Learning Model to Detect Suicidal Risk," *Crisis Text Line Research*, 2020, https://research.crisistextline.org/what-we-learned-from-training-a-machine-learning-model-to-detect-suicidal-risk-2c65f1d4d9eb.

3. "Civic Engagement and Artificial Intelligence Issue Brief," *NAACP*, 2022, https://naacp.org/resources/civic-engagement-artificial-intelligence-issue-brief.

4. "The Trevor Project's Crisis Contact Simulator Uses AI to Help Counselors," *Engadget*, 2023, https://www.engadget.com/the-trevor-project-crisis-contact-simulator-171811428.html.

5. "Artificial Intelligence in the Humanitarian Sector," *UNHCR*, 2023, https://www.unrefugees.org/news/artificial-intelligence-in-the-humanitarian-sector.

6. *IBM 2019 Corporate Responsibility Report*. IBM, 2019, https://www.ibm.com/impact/files/reports-policies/2019/IBM-2019_Corporate_Responsibility_Report.pdf.

7. "The Language Data Gap: The Importance of Data Diversity in AI," *Translators without Borders*, 2023, https://translatorswithoutborders.org/blog/language-data-gap.

8. "Compassion International," *Compassion International*, 2023, https://www.compassion.com.

9. "Audubon," *Audubon*, 2023, www.audubon.org.

10. "Paid Leave AI," *Paid Leave AI*, 2023, www.paidleave.ai.

11. "How Nonprofits Can Use AI to Increase Fundraising and Engagement," *Good360.org*, 2023, https://good360.org/blog-posts/how-nonprofits-can-use-ai-to-increase-fundraising-and-engagement.

12. "World Wildlife Fund," *Facebook*, 2023, https://www.facebook.com/worldwildlifefund.

13. "Artificial Intelligence and Predictive Policing Issue Brief," *NAACP*, 2023, https://naacp.org/resources/artificial-intelligence-predictive-policing-issue-brief.

14. "National Geographic," *National Geographic*, 2023, https://www.nationalgeographic.com/animals/article/artificial-intelligence-counts-wild-animals.

15. "Dataro," *Dataro*, 2023, dataro.io.

16. "Making AI Work for Humans," *The Rockefeller Foundation*, 2023, https://www.rockefellerfoundation.org/insights/perspective/making-ai-work-for-humans.

17. "Identifying Opportunities for Investment in Black-Owned Businesses," *DataKind*, 2024, https://www.datakind.org/ 2024/03/19/identifying-opportunities-for-investment-in-black-owned-businesses.
18. "GlobalGiving," *GlobalGiving*, 2023, www.globalgiving.org.
19. "Grantable," *Grantable*, 2023, www.grantable.co.
20. "Fundwriter.ai," *Fundwriter.ai*, 2023, www.fundwriter.ai.
21. "Granted AI," *Granted AI*, 2023, www.grantedai.com.
22. "Grantboost," *Grantboost*, 2023, www.grantboost.io.
23. "Instrumentl," *Instrumentl*, 2023, www.instrumentl.com.
24. "GrantHub," *GrantHub*, 2023, www.granthubonline.com.
25. "GrantWatch," *GrantWatch*, 2023, www.grantwatch.com.
26. "GrantStation," *GrantStation*, 2023, grantstation.com.
27. "FoundationSearch," *FoundationSearch*, 2023, www.foundationsearch.com.
28. "Grant Gopher," *Grant Gopher*, 2023, www.grantgopher.com.
29. "GrantForward," *GrantForward*, 2023, www.grantforward.com.
30. "Submittable," *Submittable*, 2023, www.submittable.com.
31. "Fluxx Grantmaker," *Fluxx*, 2023, https://www.fluxx.io/ products/grantmaker.
32. "Altum ProposalCentral," *ProposalCentral*, 2023, https:// proposalcentral.com.
33. "Optimy," *Optimy*, 2023, www.optimy.com.
34. "SmartSimple Cloud Grants," *SmartSimple*, 2023, https://www .smartsimple.com/research-grants-management-software-ai.
35. "UNICEF East Asia and Pacific," *UNICEF*, 2023, https://www .unicef.org/eap/blog/artificial-intelligence-chatbots.
36. "Distress Signals: A guide for practitioners working with children who are at risk of, or who have experienced, child sexual exploitation," *The Children's Society*, 2023, www.childrenssociety.org.uk/information/professionals/ resources/distress-signals.
37. "Lupus Foundation of America," *Lupus Foundation of America*, 2023, www.lupus.org.

38. "ADL and UC Berkeley Announce Groundbreaking Project Using AI and Machine Learning to Fight Online Hate," *Anti-Defamation League*, 2023, https://www.adl.org/resources/press-release/adl-uc-berkeley-announce-groundbreaking-project-using-ai-machine-learning.

39. "How Girl Scouts Is Using AI to Boost Memberships," *AdAge*, 2023, https://adage.com/article/marketing-news-strategy/how-girl-scouts-using-ai-boost-memberships/2497816.

40. "Artificial Intelligence for Nonprofits: Parkinson's UK Case Study," *Dataro*, 2024, https://dataro.io/2024/02/16/artificial-intelligence-for-nonprofits.

41. "American Hospital Association," *American Hospital Association*, 2023, https://www.aha.org/node/690520.

42. "SECC Video Fair," *Arizona State Employees Charitable Campaign*, 2023, https://secc.az.gov/secc-video-fair.

43. "Policies for AI and Sustainable Development," *The Future Society*, 2023, https://thefuturesociety.org/policies-ai-sustainable-development.

44. "Projects," *DataKind*, 2023, https://datakind.org/projects.

45. "AWS Generative AI," *Mission Cloud*, 2023, https://info.missioncloud.com/aws-generative-ai.

46. "New Report from AI4Giving: Unlocking Generosity with Artificial Intelligence," *LinkedIn*, 2023, https://www.linkedin.com/pulse/new-report-ai4giving-unlocking-generosity-beth-kanter.

47. "Lacuna Fund," *Lacuna Fund*, 2023, www.lacunafund.org.

48. "AI Challenge," *Data.org*, 2023, https://data.org/initiatives/ai-challenge.

49. "Now Available: A People's Guide to AI," *Allied Media Projects*, 2023, https://alliedmedia.org/news/now-available-peoples-guide-artificial-intelligence.

50. "Digital Democracy," *Digital Democracy*, 2023, https://www.digital-democracy.org.

51. "AI Toolkit: A Guide to Equitable Algorithms," *The Greenlining Institute*, 2023, https://greenlining.org/AI-toolkit.

52. "Use of Artificial Intelligence in Improving Outcomes in Heart Disease," *American Heart Association Professional Heart Daily*, 2023, https://professional.heart.org/en/science-news/Use-of-Artificial-Intelligence-in-Improving-Outcomes-in-Heart-Disease/commentary.

53. "How You Can Help Amnesty Fight Twitter Trolls," *Amnesty International*, 2018, https://www.amnesty.org/en/latest/news/2018/05/how-you-can-help-amnesty-fight-twitter-trolls.

54. "AI," *Common Sense Media*, 2023, https://www.common sensemedia.org/ai.

CHAPTER 6

Bias in AI

Strategies to Mitigate Bias and Ensure Responsible and Ethical AI Development for the Nonprofit

While learning more about bias in AI, AI ethics, and responsible AI, remember that if you want more diverse speakers, developers, ethicists, employees, board members, advisors, or founders, ask diverse people with diverse networks, and they will usually be happy to help you. For many topics discussed in this section, Women in AI Ethics™[1] is a strong starting point.

As artificial intelligence becomes an increasingly powerful and ubiquitous tool leveraged by organizations across all sectors, nonprofits seeking to harness the potential of AI must be aware of the risks and challenges posed by AI bias. While AI and machine learning algorithms have the potential to help nonprofits streamline operations, uncover insights, and maximize impact, they can also perpetuate and even amplify societal biases and inequities if not developed and deployed responsibly. By being aware of these issues and taking proactive steps, nonprofits can harness the power of AI in a fair, equitable, and trustworthy manner to further their missions and create positive social impact.

Researcher and digital activist Joy Buolamwini powerfully illustrated the pervasiveness of bias in AI systems in the 2020 acclaimed documentary *Coded Bias*. While working on a project involving facial recognition technology at the MIT Media Lab, Buolamwini discovered that the software could not detect her face until she donned a white mask. She soon discovered that the AI algorithms powering facial recognition and many other applications across industries are trained on datasets that skew heavily white and male. "When you think of AI, it's forward-looking," Buolamwini states in the film. "But AI is based on data, and data is a reflection of our history."[2]

Buolamwini is also the author of *Unmasking AI: My Mission to Protect What Is Human in a World of Machines,* and along with many of the pioneering people featured in *Coded Bias*, has deep expertise as well as lived experience in the space. A few other recommended authors, if you are looking to do a deeper dive into topics related to bias, equity, and inclusion in AI, are Meredith Broussard, Safiya Umoja Noble, Virginia Eubanks, Cathy O'Neil, Hannah Fry, and Ruha Benjamin.

The consequences of biased AI extend far beyond inaccurate facial analysis. As explored in *Coded Bias*, machine learning is now leveraged to make high-stakes decisions in domains from financial services to hiring to criminal justice. Algorithms trained on historically biased data can make decisions that systematically disadvantage women, people of color, and other underrepresented groups.

For mission-driven nonprofits seeking to advance equity and social good, mitigating the risks of biased and unethical AI is imperative. AI learns from massive amounts of data, which may invade privacy or perpetuate bias, even when using data for good purposes. Many issues can arise that interfere with human rights and perpetuate inequities.

A combination of long-standing homogeneity in the technology sector, data bias and privacy concerns, and lagging regulatory and legal guardrails have produced significant sociological issues stemming from AI bias. Overcoming these deeply entrenched challenges will require intentional effort and proactive strategies on the part of nonprofits developing and deploying AI.

As your organization explores co-creating solutions with AI to amplify impact, it is essential to implement robust bias detection, mitigation, and governance practices from the outset.

This involves:

- Establishing clear policies and ethical guidelines for responsible AI development.
- Thoroughly vetting datasets and algorithms for potential biases or asking vendors how they have done so.
- Seeking input from diverse stakeholders with varying lived experiences during all phases of the process, from ideation to implementation to analyzing outcomes.
- Monitoring systems on an ongoing basis to ensure inclusion and equity in outcomes.
- Prioritizing transparency and explainability (the "concept that a machine learning model and its output can be explained in a way that 'makes sense' to a human being at an acceptable level").[3]

The stakes are high. AI has the potential to advance nonprofit missions and maximize social good meaningfully, but irresponsible and biased AI risks inflicting significant harm. The remainder of this chapter will equip your organization with knowledge and strategies to mitigate bias and co-create with AI in an ethical manner. We will explore the current state of AI bias, advanced bias detection and mitigation techniques, ethical AI governance models, responsible development and deployment practices, and key privacy and security considerations.

By proactively addressing these critical issues, your nonprofit can harness AI's power to drive positive change while avoiding the pitfalls of biased or unethical AI.

Current State of Bias in AI

Artificial Intelligence (AI) has made remarkable strides in recent years, transforming various sectors, and offering immense potential for social good. However, concerns about bias and fairness have emerged as AI systems become more prevalent. The current state of bias in AI is a complex issue that requires careful examination and proactive measures to address.

Despite artificial intelligence's metamorphic potential, AI systems are not inherently unbiased or objective. As noted in the United Nations Office of the High Commissioner for Human Rights report, "The complexity of the data environment, algorithms and models underlying the development and operation of AI systems, as well as intentional secrecy of government and private actors are factors undermining meaningful ways for the public to understand the effects of AI systems on human rights and society."[4]

Bias in AI can arise from various sources, including biased historical data, lack of diversity in development teams, and biased assumptions embedded in algorithms. For example, while strides are recently being made to improve this, a 2019 study found that facial recognition software from major tech companies "misidentified gender in up to 7% of lighter-skinned females, up to 12% of darker-skinned males, and up to 35% of darker-skinned females."[5]

This alarming disparity highlights how AI can perpetuate and amplify societal biases and discrimination. Nonprofits must know that AI is not a panacea and can reflect and exacerbate existing inequities. While people may think of technologies like artificial intelligence as somehow more scientific or inherently fair than humans, because humans create technology, technology reflects biases and inequities society has in general.

Recognizing the current state of bias in AI is the first step toward developing strategies to mitigate its impact.

One of the primary challenges in addressing bias in AI is the nature of the data used to train these systems. As Amy Paul from USAID and Nora Lindstrom from Plan International point out, AI is data-driven technology. AI systems require massive amounts of data, and "data is never neutral, particularly historical data, as the world has never been equal and neither has data collection practice."[6]

Another key issue is the "black box" nature of many AI algorithms (rules followed by computers in problem-solving operations or calculations), where the decision-making process is opaque and hidden from users and even the developers themselves. This lack of transparency and explainability makes it difficult to audit AI systems for bias and denies due process to those negatively impacted by AI decisions, such as in cases of being denied loans or program assistance or being misidentified by law enforcement. Tracking outcomes is important, although negative impacts may occur long before strong patterns appear after the fact.

Fairness in AI is a multifaceted issue that requires diverse perspectives and context-specific approaches. Amit Gandhi from MIT D-Lab emphasizes that "fairness is not one thing – it requires diverse perspectives to discuss and determine the best approach in context."[7]

Balancing competing priorities, such as privacy and fairness, can introduce bias if not carefully considered. Engaging in collective deliberation, ideally with a diverse group of people with different perspectives and lived experiences, and deciding what is most important in each context is crucial for designing fair AI systems. This also involves forming diverse development teams, solving important problems, determining values to embed in the solution, evaluating potential impacts, and working collaboratively with marginalized communities.

Deloitte's second annual survey on the state of technology ethics found that organizations recognize the need to develop trustworthy and ethical principles for emerging technologies, especially considering the rapid development of generative AI. The survey highlighted the importance of designing tailored ethical principles for specific technological products and proactively embedding them in collaborative development.[8]

Increased diversity in AI development, better data collection and usage practices, and stronger regulation and oversight of AI systems can all be helpful. Without proactive measures to mitigate bias and protect human rights, the rapidly advancing field of AI risks causing disproportionate harm to already marginalized and vulnerable populations in society, many of whom nonprofits strive to help and serve. Addressing these challenges will require collaboration between policymakers, technology companies, ethicists, and impacted communities.

EMERGING TECHNOLOGY CONCERNS

- **Generative AI:** AI-generated content may produce biased results, such as text, images, or code, and there is a risk of perpetuating stereotypes or discriminatory narratives.
- **Facial, Voice, Emotion Recognition, or Other Biometrics:** Ethical concerns surround facial recognition technology, including its use in accessing services or locations and surveillance. Voice recognition can have problems with dialects, accents, or speakers of second languages. Emotion recognition has the potential for misinterpretations and cultural bias.

Advanced Bias Detection and Mitigation

Homogeneity in development teams and data training sets, bias in data and data privacy issues, and lack of legislation or regulation can lead to biased and inequitable outcomes in artificial intelligence and other emerging technologies.

Why does all this matter so much? Let's look at an illustrative example.

Several years ago, Amazon created an AI resume screening tool to streamline hiring by automatically filtering job applicants. However, the tool was found to be biased against women.

The issue arose because the AI was trained on resumes submitted to Amazon over 10 years, during which most applicants were men. Consequently, the AI learned to favor male candidates, effectively penalizing resumes that included terms more frequently associated with women, such as references to "women's chess club" or "women's soccer team."[9,10]

This bias highlighted a critical design flaw in the AI: it perpetuated biases in training data. Amazon abandoned the tool in 2018 after realizing it was failing to meet its intended purpose and reinforcing gender discrimination. This case illustrates the challenge of ensuring AI systems are trained on diverse and representative datasets to avoid replicating human biases.

As AI expert Julien Lauret noted about Amazon's failed AI hiring tool, "It's possible – in fact common – to fail an AI project even with mature technology and great scientific/engineering teams."[11]

Rigorous data management and continuous monitoring to mitigate bias and enhance the reliability of AI systems is needed.

Some key strategies and tools that nonprofits and other organizations can leverage to help detect and mitigate bias include:

Diversifying Technology Teams: Increasing diversity of backgrounds, perspectives and lived experiences on AI development teams can help identify blind spots and potential issues early. Having team members from underrepresented groups is critical.

Auditing Algorithms and Data: It is important to conduct algorithm audits and analyze datasets used to train AI for historical biases, skews, or gaps in representation. Tools are emerging to help scan for bias.

Promoting Explainable AI: Pushing for transparency and explainability in how AI systems operate, rather than opaque "black box" approaches, allows for a better understanding of decision-making.

Collaborating with Impacted Communities: Actively engage and co-design with communities most likely to face bias or discrimination from AI applications to understand concerns and impacts. Lived experience should inform development.

Supporting AI Fairness Research: Contribute to open-source tools, research, and standards to assess and mitigate unwanted bias in AI systems. Examples include IBM's AI Fairness 360[12] and What-If Tools[13] for probing machine learning models.

Advocating for Regulation: Back legislation that provides guardrails and auditing requirements for high-risk AI applications, such as in hiring, lending, healthcare, and criminal justice. The EU AI Act[14] offers a model regulatory framework.

Leon Wilson, CIO of the Cleveland Foundation, emphasizes the need for critical evaluation, human oversight, and ongoing discussions in the nonprofit sector around influencing AI regulation and ethics. Melanie McGee, founder and CEO of We Can Code IT, shares similar thoughts, also noting that AI can be used to help mitigate any potential bias blind spots, as well:

> I'm always looking out for bias within AI. Human oversight is essential. On the other hand, I have used AI to help me spot bias in any curriculum as another set of eyes, so to speak. I have also asked ChatGPT for student projects on particular tech topics that it would consider unbiased. Finally, I'll have AI look for biased language in all aspects of communication, including marketing materials, curriculum, and more.
>
> – Mel McGee, Founder and CEO of We Can Code IT

RESEARCH TECHNIQUES AND TOOLS FOR NONPROFITS

While some of this may be more technical, as you move further into AI, this can provide direction for leadership, IT teams, and other interested parties.

Here are a few specific open-source tools that may be helpful:

Algorithmic Bias Testing Tools

- **Fairlearn (Microsoft):**[15] Assesses and mitigates unfairness in AI systems. Provides algorithms for measuring disparity and bias metrics.
- **AI Fairness 360 (IBM):**[16] Comprehensive toolkit with algorithms and metrics for detecting and mitigating dataset and model bias. Includes explainability tools.
- **What-If Tool (Google):**[17,18] Interactive tool to explore and visualize machine learning models, understand model behavior changes with different inputs, and identify biases.

Explainable AI Techniques

- **LIME (Local Interpretable Model-Agnostic Explanations):** Explains individual predictions by locally approximating the model to understand decisions and potential biases.
- **SHAP (Shapley Additive Explanations):** Attributes model output to input features, providing insights into feature importance and potential biases.
- **Counterfactual Explanations:** Shows how changing inputs would change predictions, helping understand factors influencing decisions and identify biases.
- **Data Augmentation and Synthetic Data Generation:** Techniques used in the field of artificial intelligence (AI) to address bias and improve model performance.
- **Oversampling and Undersampling:** Adjusts class distribution in datasets to address imbalances that can lead to bias.
- **Synthetic Data Generation:** Uses generative models to create artificial data mimicking real data characteristics to increase diversity and mitigate bias.

By leveraging a multipronged approach of diversifying teams, analyzing data and models, engaging impacted stakeholders, supporting research, and advocating for oversight, nonprofits can play an important role in making AI systems more equitable. Collaboration between nonprofits, researchers, policymakers, and industry will be key to developing fairer AI that respects human rights.

AI Ethics Governance Models

While many forms of AI governance are taking shape globally, the United Nations was early in the effort, and its governance can be instructive.

> I really like how the United Nations has embraced artificial intelligence. For years now, they have had a well-publicized and well-attended annual "AI For Good" conference in Geneva, Switzerland. Near the end of 2013, the UN announced the creation of a new Artificial Intelligence Advisory Body on risks, opportunities, and international governance of artificial intelligence. They are determined to have an influential role in shaping how AI is applied internationally.
> – Sean Gardner, Forbes influencer, AI specialist

As nonprofits increasingly leverage AI to advance their missions, robust governance frameworks ensure these powerful technologies' ethical and responsible development and deployment. AI governance involves establishing structures, policies, and processes to provide oversight, accountability, and guidance throughout the AI life cycle.

One key element of effective AI governance is the formation of multi-stakeholder advisory boards. Nonprofits can assemble diverse teams that include subject matter experts, community representatives, ethicists, and other stakeholders to provide ongoing input and oversight on AI initiatives. Adding educators, artists, faith leaders, social scientists, end users, philosophers, or other nontechnical and unexpected perspectives can be valuable.

Algorithmic impact assessments are another critical tool. Before deploying an AI system, organizations should rigorously evaluate its potential societal impact, focusing on identifying and mitigating risks to vulnerable populations. This proactive approach can help surface unintended consequences and spur the development of appropriate safeguards.

Codifying organizational principles around AI ethics is also essential.

Beth Kanter, co-author of *The Smart Nonprofit*, emphasizes the importance of developing comprehensive AI ethics policies at the governance level. These policies should address critical concerns such as privacy, transparency, fairness, and accountability. Kanter suggests that organizations have board members who are well-versed in technology or trained in making ethical decisions.

Moreover, continuous monitoring and adjustment are crucial components of sound governance. Once AI systems are implemented, organizations must establish mechanisms to monitor their performance, identify potential issues, and make necessary improvements over time. This ongoing process ensures that the AI systems remain aligned with the organization's ethical standards and goals.

Technical tools can support these governance efforts. For example, model cards and datasheets promote transparency by documenting key information about how AI models were developed and tested. Standardized reporting on model performance, disaggregated by demographic groups, can help surface disparate impacts.

Strong AI governance requires a multilayered approach that embeds ethical considerations and oversight into every stage of the innovation process. It demands new capabilities and a willingness to scrutinize AI through the lens of an organization's values and mission.

Nonprofits can build a culture of responsible AI innovation by establishing review boards, soliciting community input, conducting impact assessments, developing ethical guidelines, monitoring real-world performance, and embracing technical best practices. The road ahead is complex, but with the right governance frameworks, AI can become a powerful tool for expanding a nonprofit's reach and impact in its communities.

Responsible AI Development and Deployment

Developing and deploying AI responsibly is crucial for nonprofits to ensure these powerful technologies align with their mission and values and benefit their communities. This multifaceted approach addresses technical, organizational, and ethical considerations.

One key aspect of responsible AI development is ensuring diverse and inclusive teams are involved throughout the process. Nonprofits should strive to involve stakeholders from different backgrounds, disciplines, and lived experiences to bring a range of perspectives and critically examine potential biases or blind spots.

Data plays a central role in AI systems, and responsible development requires careful attention to data collection, processing, and governance practices. Nonprofits must ensure that their datasets represent the populations they serve and do not contain biases that could lead to discriminatory outcomes. This may involve collaborating with domain experts to assess data quality, identify gaps or limitations, and develop strategies for inclusive data collection.

Transparency and explainability are also key pillars of responsible AI. Nonprofits should prioritize using AI systems that clearly explain their decision-making processes and outputs. This helps build stakeholder trust, enables meaningful oversight, and facilitates accountability. Techniques like model interchangeability, feature importance analysis, and counterfactual explanations can make AI more transparent and understandable.

Continuous monitoring and evaluation of AI systems in real-world contexts is another critical component of responsible deployment. Nonprofits should have mechanisms to regularly assess performance, fairness, and impact on the communities they serve. This includes tracking metrics related to bias, accuracy, and unintended consequences and gathering feedback from affected individuals.

When deploying AI, nonprofits should have clear protocols for handling errors, failures, and unintended consequences. This includes fallback systems, human oversight, and channels for individuals to report concerns and seek redress. Responsible deployment also demands meaningful controls on high-risk applications and processes to respond to evolving conditions.

Ultimately, responsible AI development and deployment require an ongoing commitment to learning, iteration, and prioritizing the well-being, rights, and dignity of those served. By embracing inclusive design practices, robust data governance, transparency, continuous evaluation, and multidisciplinary collaboration, nonprofits can harness the power of AI to amplify their impact while mitigating risks of bias and discrimination.

Privacy and Security Concerns

Venture Capitalist Jace Martin urges nonprofits to be security-minded when implementing AI. "Cybersecurity has evolved. AI code can be easier to crack because it's mass-produced. People can have too much confidence in it, and hackers have easy access."

A primary concern is the privacy rights of individuals whose data is collected and used by AI systems. Nonprofits must implement strong data governance practices, including clear data collection, storage, access, and use policies. This involves obtaining informed consent before collecting their data, being transparent about its use, and providing options for individuals to control their data.

Data minimization and purpose limitation are key principles to uphold. Nonprofits should only collect and retain necessary and relevant data for specific, well-defined purposes. Regularly reviewing and purging unnecessary data can help reduce risks and comply with data protection regulations.

Cyrus Kazi, CEO of Quantibly, emphasizes the importance of a consent-based trust framework and transparency in using de-identified data to measure social impact. He believes that nonprofit AI needs to set up enforceable data and privacy standards, or at least generally accepted principles, and commit to social impact without commercializing critical data.

Robust security measures, such as encryption, access controls, and secure storage practices, are essential to protecting data from unauthorized access, breaches, and misuse. Nonprofits should have cyber insurance and incident response plans to promptly detect, investigate, and mitigate any data security incidents.

Nonprofits should conduct due diligence when working with AI providers or third-party data processors to ensure these partners have adequate privacy and security safeguards. Contractual agreements should clearly outline data protection responsibilities, liabilities, and compliance requirements. Privacy impact assessments and regular audits can help nonprofits identify and address potential privacy risks associated with AI systems.

In addition to privacy concerns, AI systems can perpetuate biases and discriminatory practices if not developed and deployed responsibly. Caleb Gardner, founding partner of 18 Coffees, points out that generative AI, facial recognition, and other AI applications are already surfacing ethical questions related to their use in policing and hiring decisions.

To mitigate these risks, nonprofits must be aware of the potential for bias in AI models trained on vast amounts of data. Careful curation of training data, using bias detection techniques, and ensuring diverse perspectives in AI development teams are crucial steps in promoting responsible and ethical AI use.

Like a garden that requires continuous care and attention to prevent weeds from taking root, AI systems need regular maintenance, pruning, and weeding to ensure a healthy and flourishing ecosystem free from bias. Ethical principles provide a framework for making responsible AI development and deployment decisions.

In conclusion, nonprofits must prioritize privacy, security, and ethical considerations when adopting AI technologies. By implementing strong data governance practices, conducting due diligence on AI partners, and promoting responsible AI development, nonprofits can harness the power of AI while upholding the trust and rights of the individuals they serve.

Notes

1. Women in AI Ethics, "Homepage," accessed May 23, 2023, womeninaiethics.org.
2. "Coded Bias," accessed May 23, 2023, www.codedbias.com.
3. C3 AI, "Explainability," accessed May 23, 2023, https://c3.ai/glossary/machine-learning/explainability.
4. United Nations Office of the High Commissioner for Human Rights, "Complexity of data environment, algorithms, and models underlying development and operation of AI systems undermining meaningful public understanding of effects on human rights and society," accessed May 23, 2023, https://www.ohchr.org/en/press-releases/2023/08/complexity-data-environment-algorithms-and-models-underlying-development.
5. Joy Buolamwini and Timnit Gebru, "Gender Shades: Intersectional Accuracy Disparities in Commercial Gender Classification," in Proceedings of the 1st Conference on Fairness, Accountability and Transparency, *Proceedings of Machine Learning Research* 81 (2018): 77–91, https://proceedings.mlr.press/v81/buolamwini18a.html.
6. NetHope, "AI Ethics: 5 Reasons Why Nonprofit Engagement is Key," accessed May 23, 2023, https://nethope.org/articles/ai-ethics-5-reasons-why-nonprofit-engagement-is-key.
7. NetHope, "AI Ethics: 5 Reasons Why Nonprofit Engagement is Key."

8. Deloitte, "Deloitte 2023 State of Tech Trust Report," accessed May 23, 2023, https://www2.deloitte.com/content/dam/Deloitte/us/Documents/us-tte-annual-report-2023.pdf.

9. Robert H. Smith School of Business, University of Maryland, "The Problem with Amazon's AI Recruiter," accessed May 23, 2023, https://www.rhsmith.umd.edu/research/problem-amazons-ai-recruiter.

10. Leoforce, "Tackling AI Resume Screening Bias," accessed May 23, 2023, https://leoforce.com/blog/tackling-ai-resume-screening-bias.

11. IMD Business School, "Amazon's sexist hiring algorithm could still be better than a human," accessed May 23, 2023, https://www.imd.org/research-knowledge/digital/articles/amazons-sexist-hiring-algorithm-could-still-be-better-than-a-human.

12. IBM, "AI Fairness 360 Open Source Toolkit," accessed May 23, 2023, https://www.ibm.com/opensource/open/projects/ai-fairness-360.

13. Google, "PAIR – What-If Tool," accessed May 23, 2023, https://pair-code.github.io/what-if-tool.

14. Artificial Intelligence Act, "Homepage," accessed May 23, 2023, artificialintelligenceact.eu/.

15. Microsoft Research, "Fairlearn: A toolkit for assessing and improving fairness in AI," accessed May 23, 2023, https://www.microsoft.com/en-us/research/publication/fairlearn-a-toolkit-for-assessing-and-improving-fairness-in-ai/.

16. IBM, "AI Fairness 360 Open Source Toolkit."

17. Google, "PAIR – What-If Tool."

18. Google Cloud Blog, "Introducing the What-If Tool for Cloud AI Platform models," accessed May 23, 2023, https://cloud.google.com/blog/products/ai-machine-learning/introducing-the-what-if-tool-for-cloud-ai-platform-models.

CHAPTER 7

Nonprofits Getting Started Using AI Systems and Partnerships

Big Plans for AI – Now Is the Time

Artificial intelligence presents nonprofit organizations with an unprecedented opportunity to enhance their impact and facilitate constructive transformations. AI can create powerful, positive change, including streamlining operations and fundraising initiatives, augmenting program delivery, and strengthening stakeholder relationships. However, organizations with limited resources and no in-house technical expertise may find the implementation of AI to be intimidating.

Devin Thorpe, CEO of The Super Crowd, Inc., a public benefit corporation, suggests a measured approach for nonprofits to get started with AI. "Be thrifty. First, be budget-conscious. Don't get carried away, and invest heavily in using AI tools. An almost unlimited number of free, included, and low-cost options are available. Start with those. Pilot first. Before implementing broad-based programs, pilot them. Review the results. The formality and depth of that review will vary appropriately by the use case and the organization, but nonprofits should review every implementation of AI after a pilot phase."

But have no fear! By adopting an innovative mindset, meticulous strategic planning, and the proper methodology, your nonprofit organization can effectively leverage the capabilities of artificial intelligence to further its mission. This chapter will guide you through the essential steps required to commence your AI journey confidently. How to assess your readiness, establish defined objectives, create a roadmap for implementation, and forge the long-lasting partnerships and capabilities necessary to thrive in an AI-powered world will be discussed. Explore in this chapter how AI can assist your nonprofit organization in accomplishing extraordinary feats.

Generative AI Development Plans

This Forrester Opportunity Snapshot – a custom study conducted by Forrester Consulting on behalf of Dataiku – is based on a survey of 220 AI decision-makers at large companies in North America. While not specific to nonprofits, it gives a strong sense of how leaders are thinking about generative AI.[1]

Generative AI Adoption Plans in the Next 12 Months

Use case	Currently a focus area	Will be a focus area in the next two years
Utilizing generative AI to enhance customer experiences	64%	34%
Leveraging generative AI for ideation and development of new products or services	59%	40%
Leveraging generative AI for self-service data and analytics	58%	39%
Leveraging generative AI for knowledge management	56%	39%
Utilizing generative AI for content creation	55%	43%
Utilizing generative AI in software development	55%	44%
Utilizing generative AI to improve employee productivity	54%	44%
Leveraging generative AI for customer self-service enablement	46%	51%

Note: Percentages don't total 100 because the figure is only showing two response options from the original survey.
Base: 220 AI/generative AI decision-makers at companies in North America with $3 billion or more in annual revenue.

Source: A commissioned study conducted by Forrester Consulting on behalf of Dataiku, December 2023.

Where to Begin

The first step in integrating AI is evaluating your nonprofit's current state. Look closely at your existing technology infrastructure, data assets, staff skills, and overall readiness to adopt AI.

ASSESSING ORGANIZATIONAL READINESS

Experts like Beth Kanter often suggest starting with low-risk applications first, as your organization's leadership and staff learn more about AI. "Start with the lowest risk use case that's key to [solving a critical] pain point. Right now, it's writing and data analysis using generative AI," Kanter notes.

Cal Al-Dhubaib, head of AI and data science at Further, gives the following suggestions for starting out.

"You need three forms of AI training for your workforce–safety, literacy, and readiness:

1. **Safety** prepares your workforce to recognize increasingly sophisticated AI-generated phishing attacks, scams, and fake information.
2. **Literacy** helps your workforce to understand what to expect of AI – how harmful biases might occur, when it may be safe to trust the results of an AI solution, and what questions to ask of vendors to sort hype from reality.
3. **Readiness** is empowering individuals with skills to confidently use AI tools to perform their work – this will be specialized by role and specific tool."

To get started, you should ask a series of questions to assess where you are now, where you want to go, and how best to get there. This readiness assessment will help you clearly see your starting point and identify any gaps you must address before proceeding. Consider these questions:

- ♦ What does our current IT setup look like?
- ♦ Do we have the necessary tools and systems in place?

◆ How mature and well-organized is our data?

◆ Do we have robust privacy and security practices?

◆ Does our team have the skills and bandwidth to work with AI, or will we need additional training and resources?

◆ Do our leaders and key stakeholders buy into the potential of AI and ready to champion it?

SETTING CLEAR OBJECTIVES AND GOALS

Before diving into AI implementation, it's essential for nonprofit organizations to define specific, measurable, and achievable goals. This clarity will guide decision-making and help identify the most suitable AI use cases and solutions.

When setting objectives, consider the following questions:

1. **What are the main challenges or pain points our organization faces?**
   • Are we struggling to allocate resources based on community needs efficiently?
   • Do our staff members spend significant time on repetitive tasks that could be automated?
   • Are we lacking insights into the effectiveness and impact of our programs?

2. **How can AI help us address these challenges and enhance our mission?**
   • Could predictive modeling enable us to better anticipate and respond to community needs?
   • Would Chatbots or virtual assistants improve our client services and reduce staff workload?
   • Can computer vision and image analysis provide valuable project implementation and outcomes data?

3. **What specific, measurable outcomes do we want to achieve with AI?**
   • Do we aim to reduce the time staff spends on administrative tasks by X%?

Source: Illustration created with http://Poe.com SD3-Turbo AI Art Generator.

- Are we looking to increase the number of beneficiaries served by Y% through optimized resource allocation?
- Can we improve the accuracy of our impact assessment by Z% using AI-powered data analysis?

4. **How will AI align with and support our organization's strategic priorities?**
   - Will AI help us scale our programs and reach more people in need?
   - Can AI enable us to deliver more personalized and effective interventions?
   - Would AI-powered insights help us make data-driven decisions and optimize our operations?

5. **What are AI's long-term implications and potential impacts on our organization and the communities we serve?**
   - How might AI transform the way we deliver services and interact with stakeholders?
   - What new opportunities or challenges could arise as a result of AI adoption?
   - How can we ensure that AI is used ethically and responsibly, promoting fairness, transparency, and accountability?
6. **What resources, skills, and partnerships will we need to implement AI successfully?**
   - Do we have the necessary technical infrastructure and data management practices in place?
   - What skills and expertise will our staff need, to work effectively with AI systems?
   - Can we collaborate with other organizations, experts, or technology providers to accelerate our AI adoption?
7. **How will we measure the success and impact of our AI initiatives?**
   - What key performance indicators and metrics will we use to track progress toward our goals?
   - How will we assess AI's social impact and benefit on the communities we serve?
   - How will we monitor and mitigate potential risks or unintended consequences?

By carefully considering these questions and setting clear, ambitious goals, nonprofit organizations can lay a strong foundation for their AI journey. Remember that AI is not a silver bullet but a powerful tool to amplify your impact and advance your mission. Align your AI objectives with your overall organizational strategy, and be prepared to iterate and adapt as you learn and grow.

Embrace a mindset of experimentation and continuous learning, and don't be afraid to start small and scale up gradually.

The most successful nonprofits will approach AI with a clear vision, a willingness to innovate, and a deep commitment to using technology for social good.

DEVELOPING A DETAILED AI IMPLEMENTATION PLAN

Implementing AI in your nonprofit organization requires careful planning to ensure success. By developing a comprehensive AI implementation plan, you can align your AI initiatives with your organization's mission. This helps allocate resources effectively and establish clear goals and metrics to track progress. Your organization can envision and effectively execute an AI plan that amplifies and optimizes your impact.

> Implementing the usage of AI is not like implementing any other plan of action in your organization. There are many "unknown" variables to be determined. It is critical to assess the actual use cases within all areas of the organization in day-to-day operations, management, human resources, communications, tech development, marketing, and funding. Once these work processes are defined, then deliberately match up what AI apps, tools, systems, or services would be needed to manage or optimize those processes. Once this assessment is complete, create an AI Implementation and Operations plan to document the workflows and help execute the plan. This documentation can also help refresh and update your job descriptions, policies, security, and operations workflows and provide training resources.
> – Rock Christopher, founder SuccessCENTER.com
> and author,
> *AI Creation Apps*

A. Steps to Getting Started
- Assemble a cross-functional AI implementation team with executive sponsorship.
- Conduct an AI readiness assessment to identify strengths, gaps, and goals.

- Prioritize specific AI use cases and projects that align with business objectives.
- Set clear, measurable targets and Key Performance Indicators for each AI initiative.

B. Step-by-Step Implementation Plan
- Outline the organizational-specific potential use case needs in administration, operations, funding, security, communications, staffing, and marketing outreach.
- Define data access policies and implement security controls around data analysis.
- Once the critical needs are understood, identify and evaluate AI tools and vendors.
- Research market-leading and emerging AI technologies and compare options on sites like G2 and Capterra.
- Request demos and proposals, comparing capabilities and costs.
- Select vendors and negotiate contracts, SLAs, and support.
- Establish strong data governance and security policies.
- Catalog and clean up data sources; establish a "single source of truth."
- Ensure compliance with any applicable data privacy regulations, for example, the European Union's General Data Protection Regulation (GDPR).
- Conduct small-scale pilot projects.
- Choose one or two narrowly scoped, high-impact pilots.
- Implement, test, and troubleshoot the AI solution.
- Measure results and gather learnings to optimize the approach.
- Scale up successful initiatives.
- Develop a roadmap to deploy AI to additional teams and use cases.
- Integrate AI tools with existing systems and processes.
- Automate and streamline AI workflows for maximum efficiency.

- Communicate transparently about AI plans and potential job impacts.
- Upskill staff on AI through training programs and initiatives.
- Hire AI specialists if needed and redefine roles to focus people on higher-value work with the time saved.
- Build an AI-ready culture of experimentation, learning, and data-driven decisions.

C. **Creating Key Milestones**

1. **Create and complete an AI opportunity assessment and roadmap**
   - Conduct a thorough assessment of potential AI applications within the nonprofit.
   - Develop a prioritized roadmap of AI initiatives aligned with organizational goals.

2. **Select vendor and implement pilot project**
   - Evaluate and select the most suitable AI vendor or platform for the pilot project.
   - Implement the pilot project, focusing on a specific use case with high impact potential.
   - Launch the pilot on time and on budget.

3. **Measure pilot results and refine approach**
   - Establish clear metrics and KPIs to measure the success of the pilot project.
   - Analyze the results and gather insights to refine the AI approach for future implementations.
   - Aim for a specific percentage improvement in key pilot metrics.

4. **Deploy enterprise-wide second wave of use cases**
   - Based on the success of the pilot, identify additional high-value use cases for AI deployment.
   - Scale AI implementation across departments and functions within the nonprofit.
   - Ensure integration and synergy between different AI applications across the organization.

5. Train X% of staff to work with AI

- Set a target for the percentage of staff to be trained in AI skills and applications.
- Develop and execute a comprehensive AI training program for employees.
- Aim for a high training satisfaction score among staff.

6. Set financial goals for operational efficiency, income value realized, or time saved from AI initiatives

- Establish financial targets for cost savings, operational efficiency gains, or revenue generation through AI.
- Define specific dollar amounts to be achieved through the use of AI, such as fundraising enhancements or operational savings.
- Regularly measure and report on progress toward these financial goals.
- Monitor the economic impact of AI projects and adjust strategies to maximize ROI.
- Remember that increases in staff job satisfaction and reduced burnout, while challenging to measure in dollars, are valuable impacts as well.

D. Potential Resources Required

- AI implementation team (business, IT, data science, HR)
- Executive sponsorship and change management plan
- Upfront and ongoing investment of time and money in AI tools and infrastructure
- Staff training and recruitment of AI talent
- Strong data governance and security capabilities

By developing a detailed implementation plan with concrete steps, milestones and resources identified, organizations can pursue an AI transformation in a purposeful and impactful way. Start small, think big, and iterate continuously to unlock maximum value from AI.

New AI Partnership Opportunities

Incorporating AI can potentially open an exciting range of new funding and collaboration opportunities. Forward-thinking nonprofits are tapping into AI-focused grants, corporate sponsorships, and open innovation challenges to fuel their AI for Good initiatives.

Major technology companies are ramping up their philanthropic AI programs, offering nonprofits access to cutting-edge tools, training, and co-development support. Cloud platforms like Google for Nonprofits, Microsoft Nonprofits, and AWS Imagine Grants enable organizations to harness the power of AI at low or no cost. TechSoup offers numerous related discounted nonprofit tools and resources, and PCs for People has additional options for lower-cost used technology hardware to support your changing technology landscape.

USEFUL AI TECHNOLOGY SITES FOR NONPROFITS
- Google for Nonprofits[2]
- Microsoft Nonprofits[3]
- AWS Imagine Grants[4]
- TechSoup[5]
- PCs for People (United States)[6]

Nonprofits have an unprecedented opportunity to collaborate using AI for social good. The key is approaching potential partners with a bold vision for impact and a collaborative spirit to co-create shared value.

COLLABORATING WITH AI PARTNERSHIPS FOR NONPROFIT IMPACT

Here's a step-by-step approach to building win-win AI collaborations:

Step 1: Identify your AI partnership needs and goals
- Pinpoint the specific AI capabilities or resources your nonprofit needs.

- Clarify the social impact outcomes you aim to achieve through the partnership.
- Consider the types of partners that could best compliment your nonprofit's strengths (technology companies, foundations, academic institutions, peer nonprofits).

Step 2: Research potential AI partners and funding opportunities

- Scan the landscape of AI-focused grant programs, challenges, and corporate social responsibility initiatives that align with your mission.
- Identify leading AI technology providers, researchers, and nonprofits working on your issue area.
- Attend AI for Good conferences and join online communities to network with potential partners.

Step 3: Develop a compelling AI partnership proposal

- Articulate a bold, clear vision for the social impact you aim to achieve with AI.
- Propose specific AI projects or co-creation opportunities that leverage each partner's unique assets and capabilities.
- Emphasize the mutual value and shared learning benefits of collaboration.
- Outline the resources, roles, and responsibilities required from each partner.

Step 4: Pitch and negotiate AI partnerships

- Reach out to high-priority potential partners to initiate exploratory conversations.
- Listen closely to the partner's needs, questions, and constraints.
- Refine your proposed collaboration based on the partner's input and priorities.
- Agree on clear, measurable objectives and success metrics for the partnership.
- Establish regular check-ins and feedback loops to maintain alignment and accountability.

Step 5: Execute and scale the AI partnership

- Jointly develop an implementation plan to launch your AI collaboration.
- Establish agile ways of working that foster ongoing innovation and improvement.
- Capture and share progress, assessments, and best practices with each partner.
- Explore opportunities to extend successful partnerships to new contexts and challenges.

Collaboration and partnerships can enable nonprofits to pool their resources, talent, and expertise to better address large challenges together. By leveraging the strengths of each member of the group and each organization, goals that might seem difficult to achieve alone can be more easily achieved together.

ILLUSTRATIVE AI PARTNERSHIP OPPORTUNITIES FOR NONPROFITS

- Co-developing a customized AI solution with a technology company to better predict and prevent child trafficking.
- Participating in a foundation's AI for Good challenge to scale up a nonprofit's AI-powered educational platform for underserved youth.
- Partnering with university data science researchers to analyze the nonprofit's impact data and optimize its programs.
- Forming a coalition of peer nonprofits to share AI training datasets and models for collective impact.

By proactively seeking out and crafting AI partnerships, nonprofits can tap into a rich ecosystem of expertise and resources to realize their AI visions. The key is to approach potential partners with a spirit of co-creation, articulating a clear, compelling rationale for how joining forces around AI can expand the pie of social impact for all.

Building Your Own AI Applications for Profits

As you deepen your AI capabilities, an exciting frontier lies in building your own intelligent solutions to re-imagine nonprofit services and pioneer new revenue models. Nonprofits often hold unique datasets and domain knowledge that can be translated into high-impact AI tools.

For example, a youth development nonprofit could leverage its predictive risk modeling to launch a SaaS offering that helps schools identify students needing proactive support. A disaster relief charity could package its visual damage assessment AI into an API product for municipal agencies and insurers. The opportunities to encode nonprofit expertise into scalable, AI-powered solutions are limitless.

Importantly, developing your own AI assets creates a virtuous cycle: producing solutions diversifies your revenue, which generates further capacity to serve communities, yielding richer data to fuel even better AI, and so on. While this may sound daunting, a range of no-code AI platforms are putting these capabilities in closer reach than ever.

To succeed, nonprofits must cultivate a product mindset that includes instituting agile innovation practices and investing in the right talent and partnerships. Consider launching an AI lab or fellowship to establish dedicated capacity for experimenting with new solutions. With a spirit of creative entrepreneurship, nonprofits can become the engines of their own AI-powered growth and impact.

Accelerating Current Programs with AI Tools and Systems for Greater Impact

Of course, the true measure of success for nonprofits does not lie in developing shiny AI apps; it's harnessing these powerful technologies to advance their mission in impactful ways. AI can transform every core activity of nonprofits, from strategic planning and fundraising to program delivery and impact evaluation.

Cyrus Kazi is CEO of Quantibly, a data and social impact measurement platform for nonprofit and NGO communities worldwide. Kazi shares that implementing impact data collection, analysis, and reporting for this ecosystem enhances "capacity-building" data operations for this sector. This process simplifies data collection, integrates all relevant departments into a unified business intelligence solution, and provides guidance on managing partnerships, personnel, fundraising, programs, finances, boards, and more. Predictive AI is a growing trend in the nonprofit sector, with various research papers and pilot projects exploring its potential for forecasting. "Powerful and generative AI models [will] be capable of understanding and mathematically forecasting social trends that are often not quantifiable or even well-defined," he notes.

On the planning front, predictive analytics and scenario modeling can help nonprofits anticipate emerging needs and better allocate resources for proactive impact. To enhance fundraising, AI-powered donor prospecting, personalized outreach, and optimized campaigns can grow your support base like never before. Regarding delivering programs, chatbots, virtual assistants, and recommendation engines can dramatically scale your reach while providing highly relevant services. Computer vision and natural language processing can turn unstructured data into real-time impact insights.

Realizing AI's potential requires more than procuring off-the-shelf tools. It means fundamentally rethinking your operating model to put AI at the center. This requires redesigning key roles and processes around human-machine collaboration, with AI augmenting and enhancing human efforts. Pursuing this transformation takes an openness to change and experimentation, but the organizations that do will achieve unprecedented impact at scale.

Strategies for Scalable, Sustainable AI Implementation

As your nonprofit embarks on its AI journey, it's crucial to focus on creating intelligent capabilities that can be seamlessly integrated into your organization's fabric, becoming a permanent yet constantly evolving fixture of how you operate. The most successful nonprofits will establish strong technical, human, and operational foundations to support sustainable and scalable AI innovation.

From a technical perspective, investing in modular data and system architectures powered by flexible cloud platforms will allow you to grow and adapt your AI efforts as new needs and opportunities arise. This involves building a robust data infrastructure capable of handling large amounts of data, optimizing performance using best practices and tools to enhance your AI solutions' speed, efficiency, and accuracy, and selecting the right tools for your specific AI projects.

Additionally, focusing on the entire data life cycle and investing in high-quality, diverse, and relevant data is essential, as data is the lifeblood of AI and ensures the scalability of your solutions.

However, human and operational aspects are even more critical than technology. As Allison Fine, president of Every .org and co-author of *The Smart Nonprofit*, notes, "Whether AI benefits people ultimately is a leadership issue, not a technology issue." To make AI a fixture in your organization, staff at all levels must be engaged and equipped as citizen data scientists and machine learning practitioners in their daily work. This can be achieved by establishing communities of practice, implementing AI upskilling programs, and hiring for new AI-related roles to grow your human capacity steadily.

Moreover, your operational model and ways of working must evolve to integrate AI as an integral element of every program and service. As intelligent technologies increasingly drive key nonprofit activities, your strategy, budgets, key performance indicators, program designs, and team structures must be reimagined accordingly.

Pursuing all of these changes can sometimes feel overwhelming, but with committed leadership and a spirit of continuous learning, nonprofits can successfully navigate this transformation. Organizations that embrace these strategies will achieve significant breakthroughs for their communities served and shape a future in which social impact organizations are AI-native, data-driven innovators realizing unparalleled outcomes.

By focusing on sustainability, or the ability of a system to endure and maintain itself over time while meeting current needs without jeopardizing future generations' ability to meet theirs, your nonprofit can create a scalable AI system that delivers long-lasting impact.

Finding and Preparing the Right People, Staff, and Volunteers to Co-create with AI

As your nonprofit organization embarks on its AI journey, it's crucial to have the right team to execute your strategies effectively. This involves recruiting, hiring, and training staff and volunteers with the necessary skills, mindsets, and enthusiasm to co-create with AI or providing training to help them get there.

Oxana Vusova, social impact strategist and assistant instructor at Columbia University, explains that ideally, there would be "mandatory artificial intelligence application training in the nonprofit and philanthropy space. Make training a must for everyone entering the nonprofit or social impact fields or purpose-driven companies" so the cumulative advantages of AI can accrue for good.

This is a popular sentiment in the nonprofit and impact world right now. Beth Kanter, trainer, consultant, nonprofit innovator, and co-author of *The Smart Nonprofit*, concurs and emphasizes how many free or low-cost tools are currently offered by large technology companies on nearly any AI topic imaginable, including prompt engineering, a critical skill for getting the most out of generative AI by asking precise and sophisticated questions. "For workforce development skills, you can download training on things like prompt engineering. There are a lot of free generative AI courses on LinkedIn [and other platforms]."

Here are some key considerations and steps to help you build a strong, AI-ready team:

1. **Identify AI-related roles and responsibilities:**
   - Assess your organization's AI strategy and determine the roles and responsibilities required to implement it successfully.
   - Consider positions such as AI project managers, data scientists, machine learning engineers, AI ethicists, AI trainers, or consultants with these skills as needed.
   - Define clear job descriptions that outline the qualifications and experience needed for each role.

2. **Seek out diverse talent with a mix of skills:**
   - Look for candidates with technical skills, domain expertise, and soft skills relevant to your nonprofit's mission.
   - Prioritize diversity in hiring to ensure a wide range of perspectives and experiences that can enrich your AI initiatives.
   - Seek out individuals with strong communication, collaboration, and problem-solving abilities and a passion for social impact.

3. **Provide AI upskilling and reskilling opportunities:**
   - Invest in training and development programs to equip existing staff and volunteers with the knowledge and skills to work effectively with AI.
   - Offer workshops, online courses, mentoring opportunities, and guided projects on AI fundamentals, data literacy, and ethical considerations.
   - Encourage continuous learning and provide resources for staff to stay up-to-date with the latest AI trends and best practices.

4. **Foster a culture of collaboration and experimentation:**
   - Create an organizational culture that values collaboration, creativity, and experimentation in the context of AI adoption.

- Encourage cross-functional teamwork and knowledge sharing among staff and volunteers involved in AI projects.
- Provide a safe space for team members to test new ideas and iterate on their approaches.
- Encourage willingness to try new things and use any "failures" as learning opportunities.

5. Emphasize ethical and responsible AI practices:
- Ensure that all staff and volunteers involved in AI initiatives are well-versed in AI's ethical considerations and potential risks.
- Provide training on responsible AI practices, including data privacy, algorithmic bias, transparency, and monitoring outcomes for inclusion.
- Establish clear guidelines and protocols for the ethical development, deployment, and monitoring of AI systems within your organization.

6. Collaborate with external experts and partners:
- Recognize that building in-house AI expertise may take time, and consider collaborating with external experts or partner organizations to augment your team's capabilities.
- Engage with academic institutions, research centers, and nonprofit or industry partners to access specialized knowledge and resources related to AI for social good.
- Participate in AI for social impact networks and communities to exchange insights and share best practices, and proactively learn from the experiences of other nonprofits.

By focusing on finding and preparing the right people to co-create with AI, your nonprofit can build a strong foundation for successful AI adoption. A skilled, diverse, and well-equipped team will be better positioned to navigate the challenges and opportunities associated with AI, driving meaningful impact and positive change in the communities you serve, all while potentially increasing job satisfaction and reducing burnout.

As nonprofit author and president of Every.org, Allison Fine emphasizes, "Right now you can see how fast this is going . . . we didn't even have generative AI in our book [*The Smart Nonprofit*] from two years ago. There's a sliver of an opportunity right now to shape work and workers for the next generation . . . so much of this comes back to what leaders are going to choose to do in the future with AI to make work and workers better."

Use the suggestions provided here to generate your own insights and inspiration, begin your AI journey, and unlock the full potential of intelligent technologies for your organization and the communities you serve.

Notes

1. Dataiku, and Forrester Consulting, "Accelerate Generative AI: How Dataiku Can Help You Overcome the Top 3 Generative AI Challenges," Dataiku, Dec. 2023, https://pages.dataiku.com/forrester-survey-accelerate-generative-ai.
2. "Google for Nonprofits," Google, https://www.google.com/nonprofits.
3. "Microsoft Nonprofits," Microsoft, https://www.microsoft.com/en-us/nonprofits.
4. "AWS Imagine Grant Program," Amazon Web Services, https://aws.amazon.com/government-education/nonprofits/aws-imagine-grant-program.
5. "TechSoup," TechSoup, www.techsoup.org.
6. "PCs for People," PCs for People, www.pcsforpeople.org.

CHAPTER 8

Proposed Use Cases

AI For High-Impact Nonprofit Initiatives

Nonprofits are mission-driven organizations focused on creating positive change and improving lives. To maximize your impact, it is critical to leverage the right tools and technologies that directly enhance and scale your key initiatives.

Artificial intelligence (AI) presents an exciting opportunity in this regard. When implemented thoughtfully, AI can act as a force multiplier – augmenting your team's capabilities, optimizing processes, personalizing services, and surfacing new insights. Automating repetitive, tedious tasks enables nonprofit teams to focus their human talents on higher-value, strategic activities that drive greater impact. AI-powered tools can streamline various operational aspects, saving time and reducing costs and staff burnout.

The Independent Sector has a useful guide to help with several common challenges when exploring AI use cases: Artificial Intelligence (AI) Resources Guide for Nonprofits.[1]

Here are some potential top use cases for exploring AI tools and systems tailored to common nonprofit endeavors:

Program Delivery and Client/Beneficiary Services

- Intelligent chatbots using natural language processing (NLP) for 24/7 information and intake.
- Computer vision for accessibility (image descriptions, captioning, translations).
- Predictive analytics to forecast demand and prioritize resource deployment.
- Recommendation engines to personalize services based on individual needs.

Fundraising and Donor Relations

- Donor scoring and propensity models to identify new prospects.
- Personalized email, video, mailings using NLP and generative AI.
- Social media listening and campaign optimization.
- Virtual fundraising event assistants and engagement tools.

Marketing, Outreach, and Communications

- Automated content curation, tagging, and multichannel distribution.
- Language translation using NLP to reach broader global audiences.
- Voice cloning and synthesis for audio/video storytelling.
- Social media monitoring and response automation.

Field Operations and Disaster Response

- Drone and satellite imagery analysis for damage assessment.
- Supply chain optimization and predictive logistics planning.
- Remote patient monitoring and triage through telehealth AI.
- Automated report generation from frontline data.

Impact Measurement and Research

- Data synthesis from disconnected sources (surveys, databases, web, IoT).
- Anomaly detection on program performance and root cause analysis.

- Outcome forecasting models to plan interventions and services.
- Natural language insight extraction and summarization.

Internal Operations and Workforce Support
- Intelligent process automation for meeting notes, data entry, documents, approvals.
- Spend analytics and fraud monitoring on financial transactions.
- Talent intelligence for recruiting, skills mapping, and learning.
- Digital assistants for research, writing, analysis.

The key is identifying where AI can reduce manual effort on repetitive tasks, streamline processes, improve decision-making, personalize experiences, and unlock insight from your data. This allows you to re-dedicate scarce resources toward your highest priorities.

It's best to start with focused pilot projects that can demonstrate measurable impact and learnings before scaling AI adoption. You'll need a strategy for data readiness, model monitoring, and responsible governance, especially if you are creating any AI model in-house. AI policies and guidelines are useful for all organizations, as well as proactive training for staff and leadership about possible challenges like bias within AI or its outcomes. An AI council or other internal or external group may help lend a variety of insights and viewpoints to these conversations as you grow. AI experimentation through a balanced build versus buy approach can align with your goals and capabilities. The future will be co-created by organizations that strategically embrace AI.

Amazon has created a site to help with developing use case ideation, if you are in the early stages of determining if AI might be able to solve a challenge your organization is facing: AI Use Case Explorer.[2]

There are also many databases of tools to explore once you find the use case to solve your nonprofit's challenge. One that is well-known and has excellent video reviews is Matt Wolfe's Future Tools.[3]

Once you have found a problem that might be solved or a process that might be more effectively or efficiently addressed with AI tools, you can review various options on comparison sites like Capterra[4] or G2[5] to see which tool might suit your needs the best. Make it a habit to research any tool suggestions you find here or elsewhere, to make sure they are a fit for your organization's particular needs and situation.

AI in Administrative Tasks and Enhancing Organizational Efficiency

Nonprofits are often seeking ways to maximize their impact while minimizing costs. Artificial Intelligence (AI) has emerged as a powerful tool that can help nonprofit organizations streamline their administrative tasks and enhance overall efficiency.

"Productivity savings at the ground level – summarizing meeting minutes and notes, helping out with writing speeches and documents, drafting presentations, synthesizing transcripts" and similar tasks can create large time savings, notes Leon Wilson, chief of Digital Innovation and chief information officer at the Cleveland Foundation.

Popular administrative tasks performed by AI include:

♦ Answering common questions and providing basic customer support
♦ Content creation
♦ Transcribing meeting notes and interviews
♦ Scheduling meetings and managing calendars

By leveraging AI-powered solutions, nonprofits can automate repetitive processes, freeing up valuable time and resources that can be redirected toward their core mission. This chapter will explore various use cases where AI can be employed to optimize administrative functions and drive organizational effectiveness.

USE CASE 1: AUTOMATED DATA ENTRY AND RECORD-KEEPING

Automated data entry and record-keeping technologies are reshaping document management within organizations by utilizing advanced Optical Character Recognition (OCR) and machine learning. These systems efficiently extract information from various document types, such as forms, invoices, and receipts. Automating these processes not only boosts efficiency by allowing faster handling of documents but also enhances accuracy through continuous learning algorithms, which minimize errors over time. This reduction in manual data entry cuts operational costs and scales easily with increasing document volumes. Additionally, digitizing records improves accessibility and security, facilitating better business insights and safeguarding against data loss.

USE CASE 2: INTELLIGENT DOCUMENT PROCESSING AND CLASSIFICATION

Intelligent document processing and classification systems are vital tools for nonprofits dealing with large volumes of documents. These systems use advanced AI to process documents efficiently. AI can understand the structure and content of documents, extracting essential information and classifying them accordingly. This intelligent automation streamlines document management, making it easier for nonprofits to access and utilize critical data when needed, so nonprofits can drastically reduce the time and effort spent on manual document handling.

USE CASE 3: AI-ASSISTED SCHEDULING AND CALENDAR MANAGEMENT

Nonprofits can significantly streamline their operations using AI-assisted scheduling and calendar management tools. These AI systems can automate the arrangement of meetings, events, and project deadlines, optimizing team calendars to prevent overlaps and improve efficiency. A lesser-known benefit is that AI can analyze historical data to predict future scheduling needs, helping to manage team workloads and avoid burnout proactively. Furthermore, these tools integrate seamlessly with communication platforms to ensure timely reminders and updates, keeping everyone on track and minimizing scheduling errors. These capabilities can reduce administrative overhead across the organization.

USE CASE 4: MORE EFFICIENT MEETINGS

Nonprofits often operate with limited resources, making it crucial to find ways to increase operational efficiency. AI can significantly boost the efficiency of meetings by automating note-taking, summarizing the meeting outcome, parsing out action items for attendees as follow-up, sending out recordings and/or transcripts after the meeting, or even joining on your behalf if you can't join.

Use caution when recording meetings and let attendees know the meeting is being recorded or transcribed. It also may be wise to disable automatically sending out full transcripts to all attendees after all meetings (selecting manually case by case instead), because proprietary or confidential items – for example, portions of board discussions, financial information, or human resources conversations – may not be appropriate for all invitees. Guest speakers or people on only portions of the meeting, for instance, may not be the correct people to receive all information from the meeting.

USE CASE 5: HUMAN RESOURCES AND TALENT MANAGEMENT

AI can revolutionize the way nonprofits manage their human capital. By automating certain aspects of recruiting, such as applicant screening and initial interviews, AI-powered tools can help identify the most qualified candidates more efficiently. Additionally, AI can assist with workforce planning, skills gap analysis, and personalized training recommendations, ensuring that nonprofit staff are equipped with the necessary skills to succeed in their roles. Keep in mind that things like resume screening or visual or verbal emotional analysis during interviews have faced inadvertent bias challenges in the past, so be sure your process is well researched and that your outcomes are inclusive.

USE CASE 6: FACILITIES AND ASSET MANAGEMENT

Nonprofits can leverage AI to optimize the management of their physical locations and assets. AI-powered systems can analyze data from sensors and other sources to monitor energy usage, predict maintenance needs, and optimize space utilization. By implementing intelligent facilities management solutions, nonprofits can reduce operational costs, improve sustainability, and create more efficient and comfortable work environments for their staff and volunteers.

USE CASE 7: DATA ENTRY AND DOCUMENT PROCESSING

Intelligent data capture and processing using computer vision and NLP can automate manual data entry from forms, documents, emails, and other sources into your systems. This reduces human error and tedium.

USE CASE 8: ORGANIZATION OF RESEARCH

Nonprofits engaged in research can integrate AI to streamline their processes. AI can automate data collection and analysis, swiftly identifying patterns that might be overlooked manually, which enhances decision-making. AI tools such as NLP can also organize and summarize vast research literature, keeping nonprofit teams informed of the latest trends and findings. This speeds up the research process and ensures that nonprofits remain at the forefront of their field. Using AI, these organizations can improve their efficiency, better manage resources, and increase their overall impact in their respective areas. Additionally, AI-driven predictive analytics can forecast trends and outcomes, helping nonprofits plan their research activities and allocate resources more effectively and strategically.

USE CASE 9: STREAMLINE YOUR NONPROFIT'S FINANCE OPERATIONS WITH AI

Nonprofit finance teams often face resource constraints and talent shortages. AI can revolutionize the efficiency of finance operations by automating time-consuming manual tasks, such as invoice processing and financial reporting. AI-driven accounts payable software can automatically extract and validate invoice data, streamline invoice matching, and route invoices to the appropriate approvals based on predefined workflows. This frees up the finance team to focus on higher-value activities that forward the organization's mission.

USE CASE 10: PROGRAM MANAGEMENT WITH AI

AI can significantly enhance program management in nonprofit organizations. By leveraging AI-powered analytics and reporting tools, nonprofits can track program outcomes, measure impact, and identify areas for improvement. AI algorithms can analyze large datasets to provide insights into resource allocation, program effectiveness, and beneficiary engagement. This enables nonprofits to make data-driven decisions, optimize their programs, and demonstrate their outcomes more effectively to stakeholders and donors.

USE CASE 11: COMMUNICATIONS AND MARKETING OPERATIONS

AI can greatly enhance a nonprofit's communications and marketing efforts. From content creation and copywriting to social media monitoring and response automation, AI-powered tools can streamline various aspects of outreach and engagement. For example, AI algorithms can analyze social media data to identify trends, sentiment, and opportunities for engagement, allowing nonprofits to tailor their messaging and campaigns more effectively.

USE CASE 12: PROCUREMENT AND VENDOR MANAGEMENT

AI can extract and categorize invoices, receipts, and other financial data to support accounting, audits, expense tracking, and spending analysis. It can also assist with sourcing new vendors/suppliers and contract management.

USE CASE 13: HUMAN RESOURCES AND TALENT MANAGEMENT

From automating recruiting and applicant screening to workforce planning and upskilling, AI provides intelligent tools for more efficiently managing your organization's human capital.

USE CASE 14: IT SUPPORT AND CYBERSECURITY

AI enables predictive issue detection, automated patch management, intrusion monitoring, and conversational support assistants – reducing reliance on some external IT services, even while it may be wise to keep certain elements of cybersecurity in the hands of human experts who handle new problems daily (after using AI to augment their skills, too).

USE CASE 15: FACILITIES AND ASSET MANAGEMENT

AI-powered systems can optimize energy usage, maintenance scheduling, space utilization, and more for your nonprofit's physical locations and inventory of assets. AI can also be helpful in modeling new building projects, for example to ensure that people with disabilities have equitable and convenient access.

The integration of AI in administrative tasks and organizational efficiency presents a tremendous opportunity for nonprofits to amplify their impact. By automating repetitive processes, streamlining operations, and deriving valuable insights from data, AI empowers nonprofits to focus their resources on mission-critical activities.

Funding – AI in Fundraising, Grant Writing, and Reporting

UNLOCKING GRANT FUNDING WITH AI: ENHANCING YOUR PROPOSALS AND REPORTS

For nonprofit organizations, securing grant funding is essential to power programs and drive impact. However, the process of researching opportunities, crafting compelling proposals, and providing detailed reports can be incredibly time and labor-intensive. This is an area where artificial intelligence (AI) can be helpful, allowing you to find, apply to, and report on grants and other funding opportunities more quickly. By augmenting your team's abilities, AI can streamline grant processes from start to finish – helping you get to funding faster and scale your mission further.

Mel McGee, founder and CEO of We Can Code IT, recommends using AI to better understand things like how funders think about their grant requests, how various experts might answer questions, or other areas where a different "expert opinion" might be helpful in thinking about a question or problem. "Often I use AI as a partner of sorts. I will say 'act as an [add your expert persona here], and ask me questions, one at a time, to best understand [whatever I am interested in]. It can be an executive coach, a marketing or sales expert . . . whatever you want," says McGee. This approach works well when thinking through various grants and fundraising opportunities and how to best approach them.

USE CASE 1: GRANT OPPORTUNITY RESEARCH, DISCOVERY, AND MATCHING

AI-powered tools can continuously scan across databases, websites, and other sources to identify the latest relevant grant opportunities that align with your nonprofit's focus areas. NLP can analyze the requirements and auto-summarize key details for faster evaluation. This allows your team to quickly zero in on the most promising opportunities without spending countless hours manually searching and reviewing grant postings.

USE CASE 2: PROPOSAL WRITING AND TAILORING

One of the most arduous aspects of grant seeking is tailoring proposals to each funder's specifications and crafting a compelling narrative backed by evidence and data. AI can assist throughout the writing process in several powerful ways:

- Intelligent writing assistants can provide prompted suggestions, research insights, and language tailoring based on the specific grant requirements.
- Data analysis and visualization capabilities allow you to better quantify your potential impact through visuals and model outputs that clearly illustrate your track record and projected outcomes.
- AI text generation can help produce first drafts, accelerating the writing process. Text summarization tools can also condense your existing program materials into tight proposal sections.

USE CASE 3: GRANT WRITING ASSISTANCE

Organizations are increasingly adopting AI-powered tools to enhance their grant-writing processes. These advanced technologies assist in identifying relevant funding opportunities, effectively increasing the success rates of grant applications. By leveraging AI, organizations can more accurately target high-potential grants that align well with their goals. Additionally, these tools aid in crafting more compelling proposals by analyzing vast amounts of data to provide insights that ensure proposals are well-structured and communicate the impact of the organization's mission. This strategic use of AI streamlines the grant application process and significantly boosts the likelihood of securing vital funding.

USE CASE 4: TRACKING, REPORTING, AND MEASUREMENT

For grants already awarded, AI can dramatically accelerate and enhance your progress tracking, reporting, and impact measurement:

- Automated data ingestion across your systems and data sources cuts manual effort in report generation. AI models can analyze your program data to surface key metrics, trends, and anomalies that highlight your outcomes.

- NLP can auto-generate human-readable report narratives and visuals from your structured and unstructured data inputs.
- Predictive modeling and forecasting allow you to illustrate future impact projections or course-correct mid-grant.

By augmenting human expertise with AI's speed and analytical power, you can produce higher quality grant reports that rigorously quantify your actual community impact. This leads to stronger funder relationships and improved chances of future funding.

KEY CONSIDERATIONS AND GETTING STARTED

As with any AI initiative, a strategy for data management, responsible development practices, and human oversight of AI systems is critical:

- Start with focused pilot projects that map your grant pursuits and award requirements.
- Begin with lower-risk opportunities to validate the AI approach, measure the return on investment (ROI), and scale from there.
- Look for quick wins where existing AI/ML platforms and services can integrate with your grant management workflows.

Over time, you can graduate to more custom AI models and solutions as you build internal AI readiness. The key is taking an incremental approach that enhances – not replaces – your teams' grant expertise.

By strategically applying AI to the grant-funding life cycle, nonprofit leaders can dramatically increase their capacity to secure funding and grow their impact. Start exploring how AI can turbocharge your grant efforts today.

SOPHISTICATED AI IN FUNDRAISING

As a nonprofit organization, your fundraising capabilities are the lifeblood that powers your mission and drives impact in communities around the world. In an increasingly crowded marketplace of worthy causes, you need every advantage to capture donor mindshare and financial support. This is where artificial intelligence (AI) becomes a differentiating technology for forward-thinking nonprofits. Basic applications of AI like email personalization and social media listening are table stakes. You need to implement more advanced AI strategies and models to unlock transformative fundraising potential.

USE CASE 1: DONOR ANALYTICS AND LIFETIME VALUE MODELING

You can develop comprehensive donor profiles and propensity models by analyzing your constituent data through machine learning. These models predict future donor behavior, lifetime value, best communication channels, volunteer interests, and more. Predictive scoring allows you to hyper-personalize marketing and engagement strategies. You can prioritize your highest-value donors, identify new prospective segments, and tailor messaging for relevance at scale. This leads to increased donation flows and stronger, more enduring donor relationships.

USE CASE 2: GENERATIVE AI FOR MULTIMEDIA FUNDRAISING

Beyond basic email and web copy personalization, generative AI can create entirely new audio, video, imagery, and digital content tailored for individual donors or segments. Using NLP, computer vision, and other generative models, your nonprofit could produce virtually limitless on-brand creative assets like donor story videos, solicitation podcasts, social media campaigns, and more. You could even create personalized digital avatars powered by AI voice cloning and animation to foster deeper emotional connections with donors at scale. This multimedia approach supercharges the resonance and impact of your fundraising appeals.

USE CASE 3: AI-DRIVEN DONOR STEWARDSHIP AND SERVICE

Providing timely donor support, processing inquiries, and nurturing relationships is critical but time-consuming. AI-powered chatbots, virtual agents, and voice interfaces can offer 24/7 intelligent self-service. Beyond answering FAQs, these AI assistants can process donations, update preferences, schedule meetings, surface donor data, and route complex issues to staff – providing a frictionless, customized donor experience. By automating routine tasks, your team can focus on high-touch relationship building with top supporters.

USE CASE 4: CAMPAIGN AND IMPACT FORECASTING

Before launching new fundraising initiatives, AI allows you to simulate various scenarios and model potential outcomes. You can optimize strategies and tactics before going live using machine learning techniques like cluster analysis and reinforcement learning, typically part of specialized AI-enabled software designed for marketing, fundraising, and business intelligence. During active campaigns, AI can process a wide range of real-time signals including donation velocity metrics, campaign sentiment, paid ad performance, economic factors, and more to dynamically adjust execution for maximum impact and ROI. This predictive intelligence enables you to make data-driven decisions that maximize every fundraising dollar.

USE CASE 5: SENTIMENT ANALYSIS FOR DONOR INSIGHTS

AI-powered sentiment analysis tools indicate how people feel about your organization. These tools can continuously monitor online conversations, social media posts, and other unstructured data sources to gauge how donors perceive your brand, campaigns, and impact. These insights allow you to identify trending topics, spot potential issues, and adapt messaging on the fly to better resonate with target audiences. By understanding the emotions and opinions driving donor behavior, you can build stronger connections and affinity at scale.

While advanced AI requires an investment, the potential to massively increase donation flows and elevate how you inspire donors makes it one of the most impactful technologies available to nonprofit fundraisers. Those who start putting AI strategies into practice now will be able to scale their resource mobilization for years to come. By combining human creativity and judgment with AI's predictive power and efficiency, you can take your fundraising to new heights and accelerate your mission impact.

AI for Ethical Considerations, DEI, and Responsible AI Implementation

As nonprofits turn to advanced technologies to boost their impact and efficiency, focusing on ethical considerations, diversity, equity, inclusion (DEI), and responsible technology use is essential. While these technologies offer great potential for positive change, they can also perpetuate biases, increase inequalities, and raise privacy issues if not carefully managed. By addressing these challenges head-on and integrating ethical principles into their tech strategies, nonprofits can ensure their initiatives align with their values, promote social justice, and truly benefit their communities.

NetHope's AI Ethics for Nonprofits Toolkit[6] contains several useful tools like a facilitator's guide, workshop deck, and supporting materials.

Because the ethics guidance and related policy is morphing and changing so fast, and is a critical cornerstone of the future of AI for Good, here is a non-exhaustive list of some of the top organizations with expertise to share. They may help you keep up real-time with new developments in AI, especially as they pertain to ethics, policymaking, research, and advocacy.

1. Future of Life Institute (FLI)
2. The Alan Turing Institute

3. OpenAI
4. AI Now Institute
5. Center for Human-Compatible AI (CHAI)
6. Partnership on AI (PAI)
7. Data & Society
8. Stanford Institute for Human-Centered Artificial Intelligence (HAI)
9. The Montreal Institute for Learning Algorithms (MILA)
10. IEEE Global Initiative on Ethics of Autonomous and Intelligent Systems

Additionally, inclusive organizations statistically perform better. LinkedIn research, with additional input from *McKinsey, D&I Global Market Report, and Peoplemanagement*, highlights the following important statistics.[7]

- 60% of respondents in a LinkedIn study said that diversity within their sales team has contributed to their teams' success.
- Organizations in the top quartile for gender diversity have a + 25% likelihood of financially outperforming their peers.
- Organizations in the top quartile for ethnic diversity have a + 36% likelihood of financial outperformance.
- Diverse companies earn 2.5× higher cash flow per employee.
- Inclusive teams are over 35% more productive.
- Diverse teams make better decisions 87% of the time.

USE CASE 1: AI BIAS AUDITS AND MITIGATION
AI systems are only as unbiased as the data they are trained on and the humans who design them. Nonprofits can conduct regular AI bias audits to ensure that AI models do not perpetuate or amplify existing biases. These audits involve analyzing AI

algorithms, training data, and outputs to identify potential biases related to race, gender, age, or other protected characteristics. By leveraging AI explicability techniques and engaging diverse stakeholders in the audit process, nonprofits can identify and mitigate biases, ensuring that their AI systems promote fairness and equity.

USE CASE 2: INCLUSIVE AI DESIGN AND DEVELOPMENT

Designing and developing inclusive and accessible AI systems requires intentional effort and diverse perspectives. Nonprofits can engage the communities they serve, particularly underrepresented groups, in the AI development process to ensure that their experiences and cultural contexts are considered. By leveraging participatory design methodologies and establishing community advisory boards, nonprofits can co-create AI solutions that are culturally relevant, user-centered, address needs appropriately, and are beneficial to all stakeholders.

USE CASE 3: AI FOR DEI MONITORING AND IMPROVEMENT

AI can significantly enhance the monitoring and improvement of DEI within nonprofit organizations and their communities. AI can pinpoint areas where bias or discrimination might exist by examining employee and volunteer demographics, recruitment and promotion trends, and engagement metrics. Additionally, AI-driven sentiment analysis can track online conversations and stakeholder feedback to uncover potential issues related to inclusion and equity. Utilizing these insights enables nonprofits to take focused actions to enhance DEI, such as offering bias-reduction training, updating policies and procedures, and developing more inclusive programs and services.

USE CASE 4: RESPONSIBLE AI GOVERNANCE FRAMEWORKS

To ensure that AI is developed and deployed responsibly, nonprofits can establish AI governance frameworks that outline ethical principles, policies, and procedures for AI initiatives. These frameworks should address issues such as data privacy and security, algorithmic transparency and accountability, and human oversight and control. By involving diverse stakeholders, including staff, volunteers, and community members, in the development of these frameworks, nonprofits can ensure that their AI initiatives align with their values and prioritize the well-being of the communities they serve.

USE CASE 5: AI ETHICS TRAINING AND CAPACITY BUILDING
Ensuring that nonprofit staff and volunteers are equipped with the knowledge and skills to develop and deploy AI responsibly is critical for successful AI adoption. Nonprofits can invest in AI ethics training and capacity-building programs covering data ethics, algorithmic fairness, and responsible AI design. By partnering with academic institutions, technology companies, and other nonprofits with AI expertise, organizations can access best practices, case studies, and hands-on learning opportunities to build internal AI capacity and foster a culture of ethical AI use.

USE CASE 6: TRANSPARENT AND ACCOUNTABLE AI COMMUNICATION
Building trust and confidence in AI among stakeholders requires transparent and accountable communication about AI initiatives. Nonprofits can develop clear and accessible communication strategies that explain how AI is being used, what data is being collected and analyzed, and how decisions are being made. By providing regular updates on AI projects, sharing impact assessments and evaluation results, and establishing feedback mechanisms for stakeholders to raise concerns or ask questions, nonprofits can demonstrate their commitment to responsible AI use and maintain public trust.

Ethical considerations, DEI, and responsible AI implementation should not be an afterthought but an integral part of nonprofit AI strategies. By proactively addressing these challenges and embedding ethical principles into their AI initiatives, nonprofits can unlock AI's full potential to drive positive social change while mitigating risks and unintended consequences.

USE CASE 7: DIVERSITY, EQUITY, AND INCLUSION (DEI) MONITORING

Nonprofits are responsible for fostering diverse, equitable, and inclusive workplaces that reflect their communities. AI can help monitor and analyze important DEI metrics. These might include hiring patterns, promotion rates, employee sentiment, and outcomes from human resources processes over time, to identify potential biases and disparities. By leveraging AI insights, nonprofits can make data-driven decisions to improve DEI initiatives and create more inclusive cultures. Ensuring equal opportunities for all staff and volunteers is not only good policy, but also statistically leads to higher performance, as noted in the LinkedIn study in the introduction to this section.

While AI offers immense potential for transforming nonprofit HR practices, it is essential to approach implementation with care and consideration. Nonprofits must ensure that AI systems are both transparent and unbiased, as well as aligned with their values and mission. Regularly auditing AI algorithms for fairness, involving diverse stakeholders in the development process, and providing clear communication and training to staff and volunteers are critical for successful AI adoption.

By co-creating with AI to optimize talent management, nonprofits can build highly engaged, skilled, and diverse teams that are well-equipped to tackle the complex challenges facing their communities. When competition for talent is fierce, harnessing the power of AI for staff recruitment, retention, and volunteer management is a strategic imperative for nonprofits seeking to maximize their impact and drive sustainable change.

Blockchain and AI in Transparent Giving

USHERING IN A NEW ERA OF TRUSTED GIVING WITH BLOCKCHAIN AND AI

Nonprofits must evolve to meet rising demands for transparency, efficiency, and tangible impact from donors and supporters. Blockchain technology and artificial intelligence (AI) represent the next digital frontier for charitable organizations – providing powerful solutions to restore trust, maximize donations, and drive measurable social change. By combining the immutable transparency of blockchain with AI's ability to personalize donor experiences, nonprofits can create a new paradigm of trusted, human-centered giving.

USE CASE 1: THE TRANSPARENCY PROMISE OF BLOCKCHAIN

A blockchain is a decentralized, distributed digital ledger that records transactions securely and immutably without the need for intermediaries. This makes blockchain ideal for tracing the flow of charitable funds from donation source to final implementation. Nonprofit donors could use blockchain to earmark their contributions to specific programs or geographies and receive verified impact reporting through the ledger. Every rupee, dollar, or digital currency donation would be accounted for through an auditable blockchain trail that prevents fraud or leakage.

Beyond financial traceability, blockchain technology offers several advantages for nonprofit organizations, including trustworthy credential verification, secure data sharing, and tokenized value transfer to beneficiaries. Here are some recent examples and general use cases:

- ◆ **Credential Verification:** Blockchain can verify the identities of aid workers, ensuring that only authorized individuals can access sensitive areas or information. This helps maintain the integrity and security of operations.

- **Secure Data Sharing:** Blockchain provides a secure and immutable way to share data across different organizations. For example, multiple nonprofits working on a common project can share data without compromising privacy or security, enhancing collaboration and efficiency.
- **Tokenized Value Transfer:** Blockchain technology enables the tokenization of value, allowing direct and transparent transfer of aid to beneficiaries. This can include digital vouchers or tokens that can be exchanged for goods and services.

These examples illustrate the growing potential of blockchain technology to improve the operations and impact of nonprofit organizations, ensuring that aid reaches those who need it most in a secure and transparent manner.

USE CASE 2: AI FOR INTELLIGENT AND PERSONALIZED DONOR EXPERIENCES

While blockchain ensures transparency in how funds are deployed, AI provides a powerful capability to personalize why donors choose to give in the first place. With advanced AI techniques, nonprofits can:

- Create "digital twins" using data to model each donor's motivations, preferences, and lifetime value.
- Generate highly personalized multimedia content and campaigns through natural language and computer vision AI.
- Dynamically optimize donation channels, creative executions, and engagement strategies based on real-time insights.
- Forecast future giving propensities and simulate initiative impact to maximize outcomes.

AI also enables nonprofits to utilize intelligent chatbots, digital ambassadors, and self-service portals to foster stronger relationships with donors at scale.

USE CASE 3: GETTING STARTED WITH BLOCKCHAIN AND AI FOR SOCIAL IMPACT

Implementing these innovative technologies requires careful planning, the right partners, and a phased approach:

- ◆ Establish clear use cases and success metrics aligned to your mission.
- ◆ Inventory your organization's data maturity and readiness.
- ◆ Create a robust data governance, security, and ethics framework.
- ◆ Identify blockchain and AI platforms built for the social impact sector.
- ◆ Launch pilot projects focused on a core donor journey or program area.
- ◆ Expand steadily with an emphasis on stakeholder change management.

Responsible adoption of blockchain and AI will future-proof your nonprofit, attracting the next generation of donors, partners, and advocates seeking credible societal impact. While challenges exist, organizations willing to embrace digital transformation stand to make powerful leaps forward.

Nonprofits that cultivate trusted, transparent, and personalized giving experiences will be best positioned to tackle the world's most pressing challenges. Those who can blend human-centered innovation with radical accountability and harness the power of blockchain and AI can usher in a new era of trusted giving and accelerate their mission impact like never before.

Utilizing AI to Measure ROI

DRIVING MEASURABLE IMPACT: HOW AI UNLOCKS ROI FOR NONPROFITS

In the nonprofit sector, ROI extends beyond financial returns – it encompasses rigorously quantifying and maximizing the positive impact generated by every dollar, hour, and initiative invested in advancing your mission. Comprehensive measurement and analysis are vital for attracting funders and optimizing programs, and ultimately improving more lives. However, traditional impact measurement methods often rely on labor-intensive processes such as surveys, manual data entry, statistical modeling, and uncovering historical trends. As digital channels and engagement platforms proliferate, the complexity of measurement grows exponentially. This is where AI emerges as a new and more efficient way of doing things, empowering nonprofits to gain real-time visibility into performance drivers. Nonprofits can now precisely quantify outcomes and dynamically optimize for maximum mission impact.

USE CASE 1: UNIFIED DATA INTEGRATION AND ENRICHMENT

AI can seamlessly ingest, clean, and synthesize raw data from various sources, including via customer/client relationship management software systems (CRMs), websites, apps, communications, surveys, and field data. Nonprofits can ensure reliable measurement and analysis by creating a solid data foundation. AI models can also intelligently infer missing data points through predictive techniques, enhancing data completeness and accuracy.

USE CASE 2: AI-DRIVEN QUALITATIVE ANALYSIS

Unstructured qualitative feedback from supporters and beneficiaries holds valuable insights but can be challenging to analyze manually. NLP algorithms can automatically process text, images, audio, and video data at scale, surfacing key themes and sentiment to better understand stakeholder perceptions and experiences. This helps nonprofits with informing program improvements and communication strategies.

USE CASE 3: PROGRAM AND SERVICE DEMAND FORECASTING

AI can forecast future demand cycles. These can include donation requirements, distribution logistics, service volumes, and more by leveraging predictive modeling on internal data combined with external economic, social, and environmental signals. This proactive resource allocation ensures that nonprofits are well-prepared to meet the needs of their beneficiaries and optimize operational efficiency.

USE CASE 4: PERSONALIZED DONOR/SUPPORTER VALUE AND CHURN PREDICTION
AI can constantly track digital engagement signals across channels, providing nonprofits with real-time visibility into predicted donor/supporter lifetime value (LTV), churn risks, and behaviors. This intelligence can also enable dynamic personalization and preemptive cultivation strategies, maximizing supporter retention and long-term value.

USE CASE 5: SIMULATION AND SCENARIO PLANNING
Through advanced simulation, AI allows nonprofits to model the projected impact of potential strategies before execution. Optimizing tactics, investments, and learning capabilities can result in stronger performance. This data-driven decision-making approach helps organizations allocate resources effectively and mitigate risks associated with new initiatives.

USE CASE 6: AI-POWERED BENCHMARKING
By tapping into broader sector benchmarks and best practice models trained on aggregate data, nonprofits can gain comparative intelligence to gauge their performance against peers and identify areas for improvement. AI-powered benchmarking provides valuable context and insights, enabling organizations to set realistic goals and adopt proven strategies for success.

USE CASE 7: DATA ANALYSIS AND REPORTING
AI can automate the analysis of vast amounts of data, identifying patterns, trends, and correlations that might otherwise go unnoticed. By generating comprehensive reports and dashboards, AI empowers nonprofit leaders to make

informed decisions based on real-time insights. This data-driven approach enhances transparency, accountability, and impact reporting to stakeholders.

USE CASE 8: AUTOMATING DATA ENTRY AND CLEANING

Manual data entry and cleaning can be time-consuming and error-prone. AI can automate these processes, ensuring data accuracy and consistency across systems. By eliminating manual effort, nonprofits can redirect valuable staff time toward higher-impact activities and strategic initiatives; tasks that are more tedious or repetitive, when offloaded to AI, can in turn reduce burnout by freeing up staff for other, potentially more creative tasks.

USE CASE 9: GENERATING INSIGHTS AND VISUALIZATIONS FROM LARGE DATASETS

AI excels at processing and deriving meaningful insights from large, complex datasets. Through advanced data visualization techniques, AI can present findings in intuitive, interactive formats that facilitate understanding and decision-making, including infographics and other visuals. This enables nonprofits to uncover hidden patterns, identify areas of opportunity, and more easily communicate impact effectively to stakeholders.

USE CASE 10: PREPARING REPORTS FOR STAKEHOLDERS AND DONORS

AI can assist in the generation of professional, data-rich reports tailored to the needs and preferences of various stakeholders, including donors, board members, and partners. Automating and streamlining report preparation can help ensure consistent branding, data accuracy, and timely delivery, which in turn can increase transparency and build trust.

While upfront investments are required for data infrastructure and AI enablement, the potential to substantially elevate mission ROI – from fundraising and brand engagement to program effectiveness and lives impacted – makes it one of the most meaningful technological revolutions for social good organizations. Accurate measurement and ROI intelligence are indispensable for nonprofits navigating an increasingly competitive philanthropic landscape with evolving stakeholder expectations. By co-creating with AI to gain deep quantitative insights, nonprofits can rigorously substantiate their mission impact to the world and drive sustainable, transformative change.

Use AI to Improve Impact to Cause or Community Served

With all its use cases for good, AI can be a partner to help your organization in solving challenges that were previously daunting. Using AI data insights creatively, through open-source datasets that can provide insights that inform programs, is one way to harness this capability.

For example, Patrick Callihan, CEO of Tech Impact, describes some research uses of open datasets combined with generative AI:

> I really like the Data Commons tool published by Google. It is a tool that organizes and publishes data from various sources to provide information and insights. It is very accessible, open-sourced, and available to anyone that wants to use the data. Using a generative AI model, the user can ask questions like "how many people live in poverty in Philadelphia?" and receive, within seconds, answers that are easily understandable and also provides opportunities to drill into the data and find out, for instance, the answer to the same question by gender or race. Of course, the information is only as good as the data it is using, so at times that can be outdated. However, it is still a very reliable source for information. Nonprofits, for example, could use that data and information to respond to grants if they are solving poverty issues within Philadelphia.

At the heart of every nonprofit's mission is the desire to create meaningful, lasting change in the lives of the individuals and communities they serve. However, achieving measurable impact at scale can be challenging, especially when faced with limited resources, complex social issues, and evolving community needs. Artificial intelligence (AI) has indeed become a powerful tool for nonprofits, enabling them to enhance their impact and address critical global issues.

USE CASE 1: AI-POWERED NEEDS ASSESSMENT AND TARGETING

Understanding the unique needs and challenges of the communities served is essential for designing effective interventions and allocating resources efficiently. AI can analyze large volumes of data from various sources, including social media, government databases, community surveys, or open-source data sets to identify patterns, trends, and gaps in service provision.

Leveraging machine learning algorithms, nonprofits can understand more about communities based on specific factors, like socioeconomic status, health indicators, or educational attainment, which can help identify new ways to target outreach and personalized support.

USE CASE 2: PREDICTIVE ANALYTICS FOR PROACTIVE INTERVENTION

AI can help nonprofits move in more proactive ways for their causes by predicting potential challenges or potential risks before a crisis or disaster occurs. For example, AI-powered predictive models can analyze historical data on homelessness, substance abuse, or domestic violence to identify early warning signs and trigger proactive interventions. Nonprofits can focus their efforts on prevention and early intervention, ultimately reducing the need for more costly and complex services in the future.

USE CASE 3: AI-DRIVEN PROGRAM OPTIMIZATION AND PERSONALIZATION

AI can analyze program data, participant feedback, and outcomes to identify the most effective interventions for specific subgroups or individuals. AI-powered recommendation engines and adaptive learning algorithms can help nonprofits personalize program content as well as delivery and support methods to maximize engagement and impact for each participant.

USE CASE 4: AI-ENHANCED IMPACT MEASUREMENT AND REPORTING

Demonstrating measurable impact is crucial for securing funding. It also increases public trust and drives continuous improvement by using metrics to benchmark performance. However, traditional impact measurement methods can be time-consuming and resource-intensive or limited in scope. AI can automate the collection and analysis of impact data from multiple sources, providing real-time insights into program effectiveness and outcomes. Through the utilization of AI-enhanced dashboards and reporting tools, nonprofit organizations can effectively convey their achievements to stakeholders. These tools empower nonprofits to pinpoint opportunities for enhancement and make informed decisions based on data, fine-tuning their strategies for maximum impact.

USE CASE 5: AI-POWERED COMMUNITY ENGAGEMENT AND FEEDBACK LOOPS

Engaging the communities served and incorporating their feedback into program design and delivery is essential for building trust and driving long-term impact. AI can help nonprofits scale their community engagement efforts by analyzing social media conversations, online forums, and other digital channels to gather real-time feedback and sentiment analysis.

AI-powered chatbots and virtual assistants can also provide 24/7 support, answer common questions, and gather input from community members who may face barriers to traditional engagement methods.

USE CASE 6: COLLABORATIVE AI FOR COLLECTIVE IMPACT

AI can enable collective decision-making and secure data sharing to address complex social issues, thereby facilitating collaborative impact initiatives across nonprofits, government agencies, private sector partners, and other stakeholders.

By utilizing privacy-preserving AI techniques and federated learning, nonprofits can combine their data and insights while safeguarding the privacy and confidentiality of individuals. Utilizing this collaborative approach makes it possible to identify systemic challenges, minimize redundant efforts, and inspire collective action in pursuit of common objectives.

Although AI presents tremendous potential for enhancing the impact of nonprofit organizations, implementation must be approached with caution and deliberation. It is the responsibility of nonprofits to ensure that AI systems are accountable and consistent with their values and mission, while also being transparent. Effective AI adoption requires several key elements: active involvement of the communities being served in developing and implementing AI solutions, consistent evaluation of AI models for impartiality and bias, and provision of transparent communication and training to personnel and stakeholders.

Nonprofits can affect profound and lasting change in the communities and lives of the individuals they serve by collaborating with AI in the process of co-creation. With social challenges becoming more complex and interconnected, nonprofit organizations can strategically leverage the power of artificial intelligence to create a more equitable and sustainable world.

Using AI for Security, Privacy, and Cybersecurity

Nonprofits face growing challenges in safeguarding sensitive data, protecting privacy, and defending against cyber threats. As organizations collect and store vast amounts of personal information about stakeholders, ensuring robust security and compliance is non-negotiable. However, traditional security measures often struggle to keep pace with the speed and sophistication of modern cyber attacks. This is where AI emerges as a powerful ally, enabling nonprofits to proactively detect, prevent, and respond to security incidents while upholding the highest data protection and privacy standards.

"Data privacy and transparency have been issues in the non-profit sector long before the introduction of AI," explains Caleb Gardner, founding partner of 18 Coffees. "Often due to a lack of resources dedicated to the security of data, the collection of data without an apparent use case and without a plan for its deletion" nonprofits inadvertently create safety or security concerns that are amplified with increased use of AI by both nonprofits themselves or entities with nefarious intentions.

It is critical to examine these issues now and plan to ensure data security, privacy, and protection from cyber threats. For many nonprofits, this may be a good place to partner with a professional company that handles these sophisticated issues daily.

USE CASE 1: AI-POWERED THREAT DETECTION AND PREVENTION

AI can continuously monitor network traffic, user behavior, and system logs to identify potential security breaches, malware infections, and suspicious activities in real time. By leveraging machine learning algorithms trained on vast datasets of known threats and attack patterns, AI can detect anomalies and predict emerging risks with unparalleled accuracy. This proactive approach allows nonprofits to take swift action, mitigate vulnerabilities, and prevent costly data breaches.

USE CASE 2: AUTOMATED COMPLIANCE MONITORING AND REPORTING

Nonprofits must navigate a complex web of data protection regulations, such as the General Data Protection Regulation (GDPR), the California Consumer Privacy Act (CCPA), and the Health Insurance Portability and Accountability Act (HIPAA), to ensure compliance and maintain public trust. AI can automate the monitoring and reporting of compliance activities, flagging potential violations, and generating audit-ready documentation. By streamlining compliance processes, AI helps nonprofits avoid penalties, protect their reputation, and focus on their core mission.

USE CASE 3: AI-ENHANCED ACCESS CONTROL AND IDENTITY MANAGEMENT

Implementing granular access controls and robust identity management is crucial for preventing unauthorized access to sensitive data. AI can intelligently analyze user behavior, device patterns, and contextual factors to verify identities and detect potential impersonation attempts continuously. By utilizing features like biometric authentication (use with caution as some forms may create bias challenges), risk-based access policies, and adaptive authentication techniques, AI ensures that only authorized individuals can access critical resources.

USE CASE 4: PRIVACY-PRESERVING DATA ANALYTICS

Nonprofits often need to analyze sensitive data to derive insights and improve programs. However, traditional analytics approaches can compromise individual privacy. AI enabled privacy-preserving techniques (such as differential privacy and homomorphic encryption) allow organizations to perform advanced analytics while protecting the confidentiality of personal information. This empowers nonprofits to make data-driven decisions without sacrificing privacy.

USE CASE 5: AI-POWERED SECURITY AWARENESS TRAINING

Error remains a significant risk factor in cybersecurity. AI can personalize and gamify security awareness training programs, adapting content and difficulty based on each employee's knowledge level and learning style. By leveraging NLP and sentiment analysis, AI can also monitor employee communications and provide real-time guidance to prevent accidental data leaks or risky behaviors.

USE CASE 6: AUTOMATED INCIDENT RESPONSE AND REMEDIATION

Rapid response is critical to minimizing damage and ensuring business continuity when security incidents occur. AI can automate incident triage and remediation processes, or help with investigation, reducing the mean time to detect and resolve threats. By integrating with security orchestration, automation, and response (SOAR) platforms, AI enables nonprofits to coordinate incident response across multiple tools and teams efficiently.

While AI offers immense potential for enhancing nonprofit cybersecurity, it is essential to approach implementation thoughtfully. Nonprofits must invest in building robust data governance frameworks. It is also imperative to ensure that transparency and accountability are part and parcel of AI decision-making, and that regular of auditing AI systems for fairness and bias is happening. Collaboration with trusted technology partners and staying informed about the latest AI security best practices are key to successful adoption.

By co-creating with AI to fortify their security posture, nonprofits can protect the trust placed in them by donors, partners, and the communities they serve. Digital resilience is paramount. Harnessing the power of AI for security, privacy, and cybersecurity is not just an option – it is an imperative for nonprofits seeking to create impact in a safe and responsible manner.

Staff Recruitment and Retention – Volunteer Management

Nonprofits rely heavily on their staff and volunteers' passion and unique skills to drive their mission forward. However, attracting, retaining, and managing top talent can be challenging and strain nonprofit human resource (HR) departments. This is where artificial intelligence emerges as a partner in enabling nonprofits to streamline recruitment processes while enhancing employee and volunteer engagement and optimizing talent management strategies.

USE CASE 1: AI-POWERED CANDIDATE SOURCING AND SCREENING

Keeping in mind that this area has faced some continuing challenges related to bias, and should be used with mindfulness and some caution, AI can automate the sourcing and screening of job candidates, saving nonprofits valuable time and resources. By leveraging NLP and machine learning algorithms, AI can analyze job descriptions and resumes, and even social media profiles, to identify qualified candidates based on skills or experience. AI-powered chatbots can also engage with candidates. This can streamline tasks like answering common questions or scheduling interviews, providing a seamless and personalized candidate experience.

USE CASE 2: PREDICTIVE ANALYTICS FOR EMPLOYEE RETENTION

Nonprofits often struggle with high employee turnover. This can disrupt operations and impact mission delivery. AI can analyze employee data, including engagement levels and job satisfaction indicators, to predict which employees are at risk of leaving. Nonprofits can proactively reduce turnover and retain top talent by identifying early warning signs and providing personalized retention strategies. Targeted training, mentorship, or career development opportunities may help retain staff that were otherwise considering leaving.

USE CASE 3: AI-DRIVEN VOLUNTEER MATCHING AND MANAGEMENT

Effectively pairing volunteers with suitable opportunities is vital to enhancing engagement and impact for nonprofits. AI technology plays an essential role by analyzing individual volunteer profiles, including their previous participation and stated preferences. This allows for tailored recommendations of volunteer opportunities that align closely with each person's skills, interests, and available times.

AI-powered platforms further simplify the management of volunteer activities by automating essential processes such as scheduling, communication, and feedback collection. This automation is particularly beneficial for efficiently managing extensive volunteer networks.

USE CASE 4: PERSONALIZED EMPLOYEE AND VOLUNTEER TRAINING

AI technology significantly enhances training programs for nonprofit staff and volunteers by offering customized learning experiences. By evaluating individual learning styles, identifying skill deficiencies, and analyzing performance data, AI can suggest specific training materials that meet the unique needs of each participant.

Additionally, AI's capability to adjust the complexity of training content ensures that everyone is both challenged and supported appropriately. Real-time feedback and personalized coaching are other critical features enabled by AI, which help individuals progress effectively at their own pace.

USE CASE 5: AI-ASSISTED PERFORMANCE MANAGEMENT AND FEEDBACK

Providing regular, constructive feedback is essential for employee and volunteer growth and engagement. However, manual performance evaluations can be time-consuming and prone to bias. AI can assist in the performance management process by analyzing objective metrics and generating insights into individual strengths and areas for improvement. AI-powered tools can also facilitate continuous, real-time feedback loops, enabling managers to provide timely guidance and recognition.

USE CASE 6: DIVERSITY, EQUITY, AND INCLUSION (DEI) MONITORING

Nonprofits are responsible for fostering diverse, equitable, and inclusive workplaces that reflect their communities. AI can help monitor and analyze DEI metrics, such as hiring patterns, promotion rates, and employee sentiment, to identify potential biases and disparities. By leveraging AI insights, nonprofits can make data-driven decisions that improve DEI initiatives. This can create more inclusive cultures and ensure equal opportunities for all staff and volunteers.

The potential of AI to transform HR practices in non-profits is immense, but it must be implemented with care. Nonprofits must ensure that AI systems are transparent, unbiased, and in line with their core values and mission. This requires regular auditing of AI algorithms and incorporating diverse perspectives during development, a crucial step in the responsible adoption of AI technology.

Clear communication and comprehensive training for staff and volunteers are vital to facilitating the smooth integration and acceptance of AI technologies. By engaging stakeholders in the design and implementation processes, nonprofits can foster a sense of ownership and alignment with AI-driven initiatives.

AI's role in optimizing talent management is crucial, especially in a competitive talent landscape. Nonprofits can use AI to improve staff recruitment, increase retention, and enhance volunteer management. This leads to the formation of diverse and skilled teams well-equipped to tackle their communities' complex challenges.

As AI technology evolves, nonprofit leaders must stay informed and proactive in adopting AI solutions that resonate with their organizational goals. By collaborating closely with AI, nonprofits can achieve significant impacts and foster enduring change within their communities, ensuring they remain relevant and effective in a rapidly changing world.

Notes

1. Independent Sector, *Artificial Intelligence (AI) Resources Guide for Nonprofits*, 2023, https://independentsector.org/wp-content/uploads/2023/11/IS-Artificial-Intelligence-Resouces-Guide.pdf.

2. Amazon.com, *AI Use Case Explorer*, https://aws.amazon.com/machine-learning/ai-use-cases.

3. Matt Wolfe, *Future Tools*, https://www.futuretools.io/?ref=mattwolfe.com.

4. *Capterra*, www.capterra.com.

5. *G2*, www.g2.com/.

6. NetHope, *AI Ethics for Nonprofits Toolkit*, https://nethope.org/toolkits/artificial-intelligence-ai-ethics-for-nonprofits-toolkit/.

7. LinkedIn, *Diversity Workplace Statistics: DEI Importance*, https://learning.linkedin.com/resources/learning-culture/diversity-workplace-statistics-dei-importance.

CHAPTER 9

AI Use Cases in Marketing, Communications, Engagement, and Events

Integrating artificial intelligence (AI) has become crucial for nonprofit organizations aiming to maximize their impact and engage stakeholders effectively. This chapter will explore the potential of some key use cases of AI in marketing, communications, engagement, and events. Various applications of AI will be discussed in these critical areas, providing insights and strategies to enhance your nonprofit's outreach and engagement.

Some resources to keep up to date on the latest trends in leveraging AI for nonprofits in marketing, communications, engagement, and events that are helpful are:

Nonprofit Marketing Guide | Training, Resources, and More for Nonprofit Marketers[1]

This site offers extensive training, resources, and tools specifically designed for nonprofit marketers. It includes free courses, templates, a blog with the latest tips and strategies, and various membership options for more in-depth learning and support.

Marketing AI Institute | Artificial Intelligence for Marketing[2]

This platform is dedicated to exploring the intersection of artificial intelligence and marketing. It offers insights, research, case studies, and practical advice on how AI can be leveraged to improve marketing efforts.

Artificial Intelligence for Nonprofits: Complete Explainer – Dataro[3]

Dataro provides a comprehensive guide on how artificial intelligence can be utilized by nonprofits. This resource covers various AI applications, best practices, and real-world examples to help nonprofits enhance their operations and outreach efforts.

Nonprofit Tech for Good | A Digital Marketing and Fundraising Resource for Nonprofits[4]

This site is a valuable resource for nonprofits looking to improve their digital marketing and fundraising strategies. It offers news, trends, and tips on technology and social media to help nonprofits succeed.

Nonprofit Hub Home | Free Nonprofit Resources[5]

Nonprofit Hub provides free resources, articles, webinars, and guides for nonprofit professionals. It focuses on a wide range of topics including marketing, fundraising, management, and technology.

Think with Google | Discover Marketing Research and Digital Trends[6]

Think with Google offers insights and research on the latest digital marketing trends. It provides data-driven articles, case studies, and tools to help marketers stay ahead in the digital landscape.

Nonprofit Solutions and Technology | Microsoft Nonprofits[7]

Microsoft's nonprofit solutions page offers technology products and services tailored for nonprofit organizations.

It includes information on discounted software, cloud solutions, and other tools to enhance nonprofit operations and impact.

From utilizing AI for branding and marketing campaigns to automating social media communications, targeting, and engaging with stakeholders, implementing chatbots and virtual assistants, and revolutionizing event initiatives, gain valuable knowledge and practical insights on integrating AI into your nonprofit's strategies. By embracing the power of AI, you can unlock new growth opportunities, expand your reach, and ultimately achieve a more significant impact in the communities you serve.

AI in Nonprofit Branding and Marketing Campaigns

UNLEASHING AI TO AMPLIFY YOUR NONPROFIT'S BRAND AND MARKETING

Authentic brand storytelling and integrated marketing are essential for nonprofits to inspire action, cultivate communities, and drive real-world impact. However, developing compelling narratives and executing resonant campaigns requires significant creative effort and resources. This is where artificial intelligence (AI) emerges as a powerful co-pilot and strategic asset for nonprofit marketing and communications teams. By intelligently augmenting human creativity and execution, AI can help elevate your brand expression, personalize outreach, streamline production, enhance engagement, and ultimately accelerate your mission.

USE CASE 1: BRAND VOICE AND CONTENT CREATION
- Natural language processing (NLP) for analyzing existing brand guidelines, tones, and messaging.

- AI writing assistants to generate on-brand briefs, scripts, website copy, and marketing collateral.
- Neural style transfer using computer vision to create branded visual assets and media.
- Generative AI for producing brand characters, digital ambassadors, and immersive experiences.

AI can help nonprofits maintain a consistent brand voice and streamline content creation. NLP can analyze existing brand guidelines and generate on-brand copy. Computer vision can create branded visual assets. Generative AI can produce immersive brand experiences.

USE CASE 2: CONTENT CURATION AND DIGITAL CHANNEL MARKETING

- Automated tagging, optimizing, formatting, and multi-channel distribution of content.
- Intelligent content ideation systems based on user interests and behaviors.
- Social media listening, monitoring, content planning, post scheduling and engagement automation.
- AI-driven paid media campaign management.

AI can streamline content curation and digital channel marketing. Automated tagging and formatting can optimize content for different channels. Recommender systems can personalize content based on user interests. AI can automate social media management and paid media campaigns.

USE CASE 3: AUDIENCE INTELLIGENCE AND SEGMENTATION

- Unified data ingestion and synthesis across email, CRM, web, advertising, and business systems.
- Cluster models and unsupervised learning techniques to identify new audience segments.
- Propensity scoring and predictive modeling for audience valuation and membership forecasting.
- Dynamic audience management, journey orchestration, and next-best-action recommendations.

AI can provide deeper audience intelligence and enable more targeted segmentation. Unified data platforms can provide a 360° view of supporters. Cluster models can identify new audience segments. Predictive modeling can forecast member lifetime value. Dynamic orchestration can personalize supporter journeys. UNICEF used AI to analyze donor data and identify high-value prospects, resulting in a digital revenue increase of 50% and recurring digital donors by 300%.[8]

USE CASE 4: CREATIVE OPTIMIZATION AND ATTRIBUTION

- ◆ Multivariate testing (MVT) and reinforcement learning for creative iteration and optimization.
- ◆ Marketing attribution modeling to assess cross-channel impact and conversions.
- ◆ Real-time campaign monitoring and dynamic spend reallocation based on performance signals.
- ◆ Voice/visual search and multimodal content analysis for discoverability and engagement insights.

AI can optimize creative performance and attribution. Multivariate testing can identify top-performing creative elements. Attribution modeling can assess cross-channel impact. Real-time monitoring can dynamically reallocate spending. Multimodal content analysis can provide engagement insights.

USE CASE 5: EMAIL MARKETING CAMPAIGNS

- ◆ Automated email copywriting, subject line generation, and personalization using AI.
- ◆ Send time optimization based on individual email engagement patterns.
- ◆ Churn prediction models to identify at-risk subscribers and re-engage them proactively.
- ◆ AI-powered spam filter avoidance and deliverability optimization techniques.

AI can take email marketing campaigns to new heights. Automated copywriting and personalization can create compelling, individualized emails at scale. Send time optimization can increase open rates. Churn prediction can proactively re-engage at-risk subscribers. AI-powered techniques can improve deliverability.

USE CASE 6: MARKETING AND COMMUNICATION PLANS AND PROJECTIONS

- Automated generation of comprehensive marketing plans using AI planning and optimization.
- Predictive goal setting and forecasting models built on historical campaign data.
- AI-assisted media buying and budget allocation recommendations.

AI can streamline marketing planning and projections. Automated marketing plan generation can save time and optimize tactics. Predictive forecasting can set realistic goals. Simulations can project performance ranges. AI can optimize media buying and budget allocation.

USE CASE 7: MARKETING EFFECTIVENESS MEASUREMENT AND REPORTING

- Automated data integration and harmonization across all marketing touchpoints.
- Unified marketing dashboards with AI-powered insights and anomaly detection.
- Natural language generation for executive summary reports and donor communications.
- Prescriptive analytics and AI-driven recommendations for optimization opportunities.

AI can enhance marketing effectiveness measurement and reporting. Automated data integration can provide a unified view of performance. AI-powered dashboards can surface actionable insights. Natural language generation can automate reporting. Prescriptive analytics can provide optimization recommendations.

The applications are wide-ranging and powerful. From automating tedious production tasks to generating hyper-personalized creatives at scale to advanced multimodal analytics that surface transformative insights, AI empowers smarter brand storytelling and targeted engagement.

It's important to approach AI brand and marketing initiatives in phases – identifying key priorities, building centralized data platforms, establishing governance and ethics frameworks, and methodically piloting use cases. You'll also want to cultivate strategic AI enablement partnerships.

Those nonprofits actively co-creating with AI to reimagine marketing strategies will increase higher-level awareness and support. Now is the time to begin exploring how AI can amplify your brand's vital voice and stories in ways that motivate communities to act.

Social Media and Communication Automation

MASTERING NONPROFIT SOCIAL MEDIA AND COMMUNICATIONS WITH AI AUTOMATION

Social media and multichannel communications are vital for nonprofits to raise awareness, inspire action, cultivate communities, and drive real-world impact. However, developing strategic narratives while executing resonant, personalized campaigns across numerous platforms can quickly drain precious resources. This is where artificial intelligence (AI) emerges as a powerful enabling technology. AI can help nonprofit marketing and communications teams elevate their social media mastery and supporter engagement by selectively automating repetitive tasks and processes and augmenting strategic decision-making. Let's explore compelling proposed use cases for leveraging AI across various nonprofit communications functions.

USE CASE 1: SOCIAL CONTENT STRATEGY AND CREATION

- Social listening and audience analysis using NLP.
- AI-assisted copywriting, scripting, and content brief creation for campaigns.
- Generative AI models for producing on-brand visuals, videos, and creative assets at scale.
- Video intelligence for auto-captioning, translation, and optimizing social video performance.
- AI can revolutionize social content strategy and creation.
- NLP can analyze audience conversations to inform content themes.
- AI-assisted copywriting can generate compelling campaign briefs and scripts.
- Generative AI can produce on-brand visuals and videos at scale.
- Video intelligence can optimize social video performance.

USE CASE EXAMPLES: CONTENT CREATION

AI can help nonprofits create compelling content more efficiently. Machine learning algorithms can assist with researching and writing articles, social media posts, newsletters, and other content by generating relevant topic ideas, outlines, and draft versions, allowing nonprofit marketers and communicators to produce more content in less time. AI can also help personalize and target content by analyzing supporter data and determining the most relevant topics for each audience segment. By streamlining the content creation process, AI enables nonprofits to engage supporters more frequently and effectively.

USE CASE EXAMPLE: AI AND CONTENT ANALYSIS

AI provides invaluable assistance in analyzing a nonprofit's content and communications performance. NLP can rapidly process large volumes of responses and comments on social media posts, articles, emails, and more to identify common themes, sentiments, questions, and concerns among supporters. Computer vision can examine engagement with visual content like images and videos. These AI-driven insights help nonprofits understand what content resonates with different audiences and adapt their communications strategies accordingly. AI analysis provides a deeper understanding of supporter responses that would be difficult to match manually.

USE CASE 2: SOCIAL MEDIA MANAGEMENT AND PUBLISHING

- AI content curation, tagging, formatting, scheduling, and multichannel distribution.
- Automated community management through intelligent moderation and response tools.
- Social media monitoring and sentiment analysis to guide engagement tactics.
- Testing and optimization of creative assets and audience targeting using machine learning.

AI can streamline social media management and publishing in many ways, with multiple benefits. Automated content curation and scheduling can save time and ensure consistency. Intelligent moderation tools can assist with community management. Sentiment analysis can guide engagement tactics. Machine learning can optimize creative performance and audience targeting. New tools are rapidly becoming available to help with these and additional needs.

USE CASE 3: EMAIL AND MESSAGING PERSONALIZATION

- Content segmentation, dynamic audience creation, and journey mapping, AI-powered subject line and message copy optimization for increased open/click rates, and Intelligent nurturing based on individual engagement signals and propensity scores.
- Automated nurture emails, text sequences, retargeting, and up/cross-sell recommendations.

AI can take email and messaging personalization to new heights. Content segmentation and dynamic audience creation can tailor communications. AI-optimized subject lines and copy can boost engagement rates. Intelligent nurturing can adapt to individual behaviors. Automated sequences can guide supporters through personalized journeys.

USE CASE 4: COMMUNICATIONS WORKFLOW AUTOMATION

- Intelligent chatbots and virtual assistants for inquiries and self-service.
- Auto-generating transcripts, summaries, and insights from recorded calls and meetings.
- Documentation, knowledge base creation, and FAQ automation.
- Task prioritization, approvals, notifications, and campaign management flows.
- Automation of various communications workflows to boost efficiency.
- Intelligent chatbots can handle routine inquiries and provide self-service options.
- Transcription and summarization of meetings, generating actionable insights.
- Automation of documentation, knowledge bases, and FAQs.
- Streamlining task prioritization, approvals, and campaign management.

Combining AI automation with your team's strategic communications expertise allows you to streamline laborious processes and maximize time spent on higher-value messaging and audience engagement. AI becomes a force multiplier across all phases: insights, creation, deployment, optimization, and measurement.

It's critical to define clear use cases aligned with communications goals, integrate disparate systems and data sources, apply responsible development practices, and validate outputs with human oversight. An iterative approach allows you to steadily scale AI automation across social, email, chat/messaging, and content pipelines.

USE CASE 5: LANGUAGE TRANSLATION

Organizations, like Translators without Borders, use AI to translate content into multiple languages, helping to reach a wider audience and improve access to information. Language translation also includes considering how people with disabilities can access your information. For example, NLP leverages voice recognition by understanding and interpreting human language in mobile apps. This allows for more conversational and natural interactions with technology and makes digital content more accessible for people who struggle with reading and writing or who have cognitive disabilities.

Actively co-creating with AI can amplify communications, increasing reach, resonance, mobilization, and understanding. Now is the ideal time to explore embedding AI throughout your marketing technology stack and processes.

Stakeholders – Personalization, Targeting Donors, Supporters, Partnerships, and Collaboration

> One of the top ways nonprofits can use AI is to design products and services that can address the needs of diverse populations, accounting for their cultural, religious, and language needs. By utilizing AI-driven insights, nonprofits can understand the nuanced service demand based on demographics and tweak their services accordingly.
>
> – Cyrus Kazi, CEO, Quantibly

THE POWER OF PERSONALIZATION AT SCALE: HOW AI HELPS NONPROFITS CULTIVATE DEEPER CONNECTIONS

Garnering attention and resonating with supporters is an increasing challenge for nonprofit organizations. Generic, one-size-fits-all outreach simply doesn't cut through the clutter anymore. The most successful nonprofits understand the power of personalization including tailored messaging, services, and experiences for advocates, donors, volunteers, and beneficiaries. Personalized engagement fosters authentic human connections that inspire action.

Personalization usages can include:

- Personalized donation appeals and thank-you messages using AI-powered platforms like DonorPerfect.
- AI-driven donor segmentation and targeting for maximizing engagement and conversion rates.
- Predictive modeling to identify potential major donors and tailor cultivation strategies.

However, true personalization requires a deep, data-driven understanding of each constituent at an individual level and customizing interactions accordingly. This is not scalable through manual efforts and traditional tactics alone; especially as digital platforms and channels exponentially increase. This is where AI emerges as an indispensable enabler for personalization at scale across entire constituent bases. By intelligently automating processes and augmenting strategic decision-making, AI allows nonprofits to cultivate contextualized one-to-one relationships that strengthen mission impact efficiently.

USE CASE 1: DONOR ENGAGEMENT

AI can transform donor engagement for nonprofits by enabling highly personalized and responsive interactions at scale. Machine learning algorithms analyze vast amounts of donor data to predict individual preferences, behaviors, and propensities. This allows nonprofits to tailor outreach, content, and appeals to each donor's unique profile, making them feel truly known and valued. AI-powered chatbots and virtual assistants can provide instant, context-aware responses to donor inquiries and feedback 24/7, enhancing convenience and satisfaction. Predictive models can forecast future donor actions, such as churn risk or likelihood to give, enabling proactive cultivation. By delivering exceptional relevance and responsiveness, AI helps nonprofits build deeper, more loyal relationships with donors, ultimately driving increased giving and retention. While some AI donor engagement capabilities require technical expertise to implement, more and more nonprofit software platforms are embedding these features, putting the power of AI within reach for organizations of all sizes.

USE CASE 2: UNIFIED SUPPORTER INTELLIGENCE

By researching, ingesting, and synthesizing constituent data across all sources into AI-powered platforms, nonprofits can create robust unified profiles encompassing demographics, preferences, interests, behaviors, content affinity, and propensity scores. This provides a rich personalization data foundation. AI can identify patterns, correlations, and insights that would be impossible to discern manually, enabling highly targeted segmentation and outreach.

USE CASE 3: PREDICTIVE SUPPORTER SEGMENTATION

AI-powered supporter segmentation uses machine learning to analyze extensive data on supporters' behaviors, preferences, and characteristics, enabling nonprofits to dynamically group supporters into distinct segments. This allows for highly targeted messaging across communications. Appeals that resonate with each segment's unique attributes can boost response rates, donations, and long-term supporter loyalty and value.

Specialized software solutions make this AI capability more accessible to nonprofits by embedding machine learning segmentation into their CRM and marketing automation platforms. However, larger nonprofits with data science staff may still choose to build custom models. Either way, AI-enhanced segmentation is becoming an increasingly essential tool for nonprofits to understand and connect with supporters in a more personalized and effective way.

USE CASE 4: ADAPTIVE JOURNEY ORCHESTRATION

AI decision engines can adapt and map out the optimal journey experiences for each segment or individual supporter
across various touch points – website, apps, emails, events,
outreach, and more. AI monitors real-time signals to course-
correct or accelerate the journey as needed. For example, if a
supporter frequently engages with advocacy content but not
fundraising appeals, the AI can prioritize opportunities to act
versus donating.

USE CASE 5: GENERATIVE AND RECOMMENDATION CONTENT

Leveraging AI language models, computer vision, recommendation engines, or software that does this, nonprofits can
generate personalized communications and content recommendations and nurture tracks on demand and at scale across
every channel and medium. This could include crafting individualized email subject lines, social media ad creative, landing
page copy, and next-best content or product suggestions based
on a supporter's specific profile and behaviors.

USE CASE 6: INTELLIGENT SELF-SERVICE AND SUPPORT

AI-powered chatbots, virtual assistants, voice interfaces, and
knowledge management tools enable supporters to access
tailored information, services, answers, and advocacy opportunities through seamless self-service experiences. By automating these interactions and personalizing them to each
user's context, nonprofits can provide efficient and satisfy-
ing support while saving staff time for higher-value relationship building.

Technological capabilities are essential for personalization. So is a steadfast commitment to ethical data practices,
transparency, and human-centered design. AI personalization
efforts must enhance, not undermine, trust with supporters.
By systematically co-creating personalized engagement strategies with AI, forward-thinking nonprofits will foster enduring, meaningful relationships that unite supporters behind their

vital missions. In our distracted age, personalization separates organizations creating real impact from those lost in the noise.

USE CASE 7: PERSONALIZED RECOMMENDATIONS

AI can significantly enhance personalized recommendations for supporters of nonprofits by analyzing their interactions, preferences, and behaviors. Machine learning algorithms sift through vast amounts of data to identify patterns and trends that inform what content or donation opportunities might resonate most with each person. For example, AI can recommend specific volunteer activities based on past involvement, suggest relevant articles or updates aligned with a supporter's interests, or tailor fundraising appeals to match their giving history and capacity. This level of personalization makes supporters feel more connected and valued, increasing their engagement and likelihood to contribute. Nonprofit CRM systems and marketing platforms increasingly integrate AI-driven recommendation engines, making these sophisticated capabilities accessible even to organizations without deep technical expertise. By delivering highly relevant and individualized experiences, AI helps nonprofits build stronger relationships with their supporters, driving engagement and long-term loyalty.

Chatbots – Virtual Assistants for Nonprofit Engagement

Facing today's digital landscape, nonprofit organizations viscerally feel the challenge of engaging supporters across various channels while maintaining personalized, timely service. As interactions span websites, apps, emails, chat, voice, and more, even the most dedicated teams can quickly become overwhelmed. This is where AI-powered virtual assistants emerge as a new and ideal solution, enabling nonprofits to cultivate rich engagement while optimizing staff resources and operational costs. Let's explore how these intelligent conversational interfaces can revolutionize supporter experiences and amplify mission impact.

USE CASE 1: INTELLIGENT SELF-SERVICE AND AUTOMATED SUPPORT

Virtual assistants (VAs) can serve as the first line of engagement, instantly addressing common questions related to programs, events, membership, donations, volunteering, hours, and more. By seamlessly retrieving information from backend knowledge bases, VAs provide swift, accurate support 24/7. For complex issues, they can collect pertinent details, open support tickets, route inquiries to the appropriate staff with full contextual history and answer common questions. This enhances agent productivity and supporter satisfaction.

Allison Fine, president of Every.org and co-author of *The Smart Nonprofit* has a suggestion and word of caution: be sure to ask your stakeholders how they *feel* when using new tools, like virtual assistants. She says, "I think an area where we could be doing a much better job is inviting our end users, whether they're clients, donors, volunteers, or external stakeholders, into helping co-create these applications." She points out that the frantic pace of trying to keep and find new donors, administrative tasks, managing multiple grants, and other constant high-paced activities can leave little time for feedback, but feedback is critical. She explains that even with good intentions, nonprofits cannot often engage in discussions with stakeholders and tend to make assumptions about how new technology will be perceived by them. For example, imagine you're an organization that receives numerous questions, like a community center. People frequently ask about your hours or event times, even if you have all the FAQs on your website. You might think a chatbot could solve this issue. The next step would be to gather some members on a Zoom call to ask how they would feel about this solution. It's important to ensure that anyone interacting with the chatbot knows it's a chatbot. "I want the chatbot to introduce itself clearly, saying, 'Hi, I am Bob, your chatbot. Here's what I do,' so people understand and have clear expectations about the technology," adds Fine.

USE CASE 2: PERSONALIZED DONOR AND BENEFICIARY EXPERIENCES

VAs can unlock concierge-like experiences at scale for major donors and high-value supporters. They can provide tailored recognition, convey customized impact reports, make smart recommendations based on interests, facilitate donations, update preferences, and more. Similarly, VAs can guide beneficiaries through aid applications, provide multilingual assistance, track case updates, and offer personalized support, ensuring no one is left behind.

USE CASE 3: CONTENT AND PROGRAM DISCOVERY

As knowledgeable ambassadors, VAs can proactively showcase relevant content, programs, events, and opportunities based on each supporter's profile, interests, and conversations. Powered by machine learning, they continuously refine recommendations over time, driving deeper engagement and participation. Nonprofits can effectively surface high-value content and inspire action at the right moments.

USE CASE 4: INTELLIGENT VOICE INTERACTIONS

Virtual assistants enable intuitive voice-based self-service by combining NLP with generative AI models. This can include interactions across smart speakers and mobile apps, voice-enabled devices, and other methods yet to be known. Supporters can access information, make donations, sign up for events, and more using natural, conversational commands. Voice assistants like Alexa Skills or Google Actions provide hands-free engagement, expanding reach and accessibility.

USE CASE 5: MULTIMEDIA AND MULTIMODAL ENGAGEMENT

Cutting-edge computer vision and multimodal AI models allow virtual assistants to intelligently engage via imagery, video, augmented reality (AR), and more. Nonprofits can create immersive, interactive experiences that bring their stories and impact to life. For example, VAs can guide supporters through virtual exhibits, provide AR overlays for educational content, or generate personalized video messages. These multimedia capabilities unlock new dimensions of engagement and emotional connection.

To make virtual assistants a reality, nonprofits must focus on key enablers such as rich knowledge repositories, quality training data, and robust security and governance frameworks. Adopting an agile, iterative VA development and training approach ensures continuous enhancement and alignment with evolving supporter needs.

AI-driven virtual assistants provide an always-available, cost-effective engagement layer that complements human efforts. They empower nonprofits to deliver frictionless, personalized service globally while freeing up staff to focus on high-impact initiatives. As virtual assistants become more sophisticated, they will play an increasingly pivotal role in attracting and retaining multi-generational supporters.

Organizations that embrace intelligent virtual assistants are better positioned to meet soaring engagement demands and ultimately drive deeper community participation in their vital missions. The future of nonprofit engagement is conversational, personalized, and powered by AI. Is your organization ready to harness the potential of virtual assistants?

AI in Event Initiatives

AMPLIFYING YOUR NONPROFIT EVENTS WITH AI: PROPOSED USE CASES

For nonprofit organizations, events are pivotal for fundraising, raising awareness, cultivating communities, and ultimately driving mission impact. However, planning and executing successful events requires significant time and resources across logistics, marketing, engagement, and follow-up. This area is ripe for exploring AI tools and strategies. By augmenting human expertise with intelligent technologies, nonprofits can streamline processes, personalize attendee experiences, maximize outcomes, and gain powerful new insights. Let's explore some compelling proposed use cases for leveraging AI across the nonprofit event life cycle.

Use Case 1: Event Planning and Promotion

- NLP for analyzing trends, topics, and speakers to shape event themes.
- Forecasting tools to predict attendance based on historical data and market signals.
- Dynamic pricing recommendation engines for tickets and sponsorship packages.
- Automated creative copywriting, imagery, and video generation for promotional campaigns.
- Social listening and targeted digital advertising using AI audience modeling.

By harnessing AI in the planning and promotion phase, nonprofits can create more resonant event themes, optimize pricing and sponsorship strategies, and reach target audiences with personalized, compelling campaigns.

Use Case 2: Registration and Attendee Communications

- Intelligent chatbots and voice assistants for answering queries and facilitating registration.
- Automated referral code generation and management using unique identifiers.
- Personalized registration confirmation sequences triggered by user preferences.
- Dynamic reminder emails and retargeting campaigns powered by machine learning.

AI can significantly streamline the registration process and enhance attendee communications. Intelligent chatbots can handle common queries, freeing staff time for more complex tasks. Personalized confirmations and reminders based on user preferences can boost attendance and engagement.

Use Case 3: Event Experience and Engagement

- Computer vision for facial recognition check-in, or matched networking recommendations. (Caveat: facial recognition software varies greatly in accuracy and may be better used at a later date; this is an area to watch for progress but should improve rapidly.)
- Real-time speech transcription, translation, and captioning for accessibility.
- Presenter coaching AIs to enhance public speaking skills and audience rapport.
- Gamification tools and interactive digital experiences guided by attendee interests.
- Automated photo/video capture, curation, and sharing through APIs.

AI can elevate the attendee experience during the event and foster deeper engagement. Facial recognition can potentially streamline check-in. AI can enable personalized networking recommendations. Real-time transcription and translation can make sessions more accessible.

Use Case 4: Post-Event Analysis and Follow-Up

- Voice-to-text transcription and analysis of session recordings for insight mining.
- Automated nurture campaigns and sponsorship reporting using natural language generation.
- Churn prediction models to identify attendees at risk of lapsing involvement.
- Interactive data visualizations from attendee surveys, social media buzz, and business impact metrics.
- AI-powered presenter performance assessments and coaching opportunities.

After the event concludes, AI can help nonprofits derive valuable insights that can improve future events and help nurture long-term relationships. Automated transcription and analysis of session recordings can surface key themes and takeaways. Churn prediction models can identify at-risk attendees for targeted re-engagement. AI-generated reports and visualizations can convey the impact of events to stakeholders. Ultimately, AI can augment talented nonprofit event staff's skills to streamline learning, enabling even better future events.

The possibilities are expansive when considering the many AI techniques available – from machine learning and natural language to vision, speech, planning, and robotics. The key is aligning use cases to your event goals and audience needs. Implementing AI for events requires strategic data integration across disparate systems, adherence to privacy best practices, responsible development principles, and staff insights to make the most of it. However, the potential impact could be valuable because of lowering costs and boosting fundraising to create highly memorable, personalized attendee journeys that inspire action.

Forward-thinking nonprofits willing to begin piloting AI now will be well-positioned to elevate their events into profoundly engaging, intelligent experiences that propel their vital missions forward. By co-creating with AI, organizations can amplify the impact of their events and accelerate positive change in the world.

Notes

1. Nonprofit Marketing Guide, *Training, Resources and More for Nonprofit Marketers*, Nonprofit Marketing Guide, http://nonprofitmarketingguide.com.
2. Marketing AI Institute, *Artificial Intelligence for Marketing*, Marketing AI Institute, http://marketingaiinstitute.com.
3. Dataro, *Artificial Intelligence for Nonprofits: Complete Explainer*, Dataro, 16 Feb 2024, dataro.io/2024/02/16/artificial-intelligence-for-nonprofits/.

4. Nonprofit Tech for Good, *A Digital Marketing and Fundraising Resource for Nonprofits*, Nonprofit Tech for Good, nptechforgood.com.

5. Nonprofit Hub, *Home | Free Nonprofit Resources*, Nonprofit Hub, nonprofithub.org.

6. Think with Google, *Discover Marketing Research and Digital Trends*, Google, thinkwithgoogle.com.

7. Microsoft Nonprofits. *Nonprofit Solutions and Technology*, Microsoft, http://www.microsoft.com/en-us/nonprofits?acti vetab=pivot1%3aprimaryr2.

8. Tobes Kelly, "How Fundraise Up Helped UNICEF USA Increase Digital Revenue by 50% and Recurring Digital Donors by 300%," Case Study, n.d., https://engage.fundraiseup.com/hubfs/Case%20Studies/Fundraise%20Up%20UNICEF%20 USA%20Case%20Study.pdf.

CHAPTER 10

Conclusion

In the intricate social impact ecosystem, nonprofits can be likened to butterflies, flitting gracefully from one community need to another, spreading hope and resources. Just as butterflies benefit from the presence of hummingbirds, which aid in pollination, nonprofits stand to gain immensely from the strategic integration of AI technologies. With their precision and agility, hummingbirds symbolize AI's capability to sift through vast amounts of data and provide critical insights, ensuring that nonprofits can operate more efficiently and effectively. This symbiotic relationship demonstrates that when nonprofits (butterflies) and AI (hummingbirds) work in harmony, they can create a thriving environment of support and growth.

The beauty of this analogy lies not only in the complementary roles of these creatures but also in their synergy. Hummingbirds and butterflies help plants reproduce by transferring pollen, leading to the growth of fruits, seeds, and new plants. Similarly, AI, when thoughtfully integrated into nonprofit operations, can help these organizations plant the seeds of new initiatives, nurture the growth of their capabilities, and ultimately bear the fruit of increased social impact. By embracing the delicate dance between technology and human compassion, nonprofits can harness the power of AI to navigate their challenges with grace and adaptability, driving meaningful social change and fostering a more vibrant and resilient community.

As we explored in the introduction, the metaphor of AI as a hummingbird captures the essence of its role in the nonprofit sector – agile, precise, and capable of navigating complex environments. Just as we began our journey with the image of the hummingbird, we now see how this analogy extends to illustrate the collaborative and transformative potential of AI and nonprofits working together. We can create a more effective and compassionate world by drawing on the strengths of both technology and human-centered approaches.

This book examined AI's potential to help people in the nonprofit sector in similar symbiotic ways, ultimately improving the entire ecosystem.

The insights and experiences shared by nonprofit leaders and AI experts, as well as comprehensive research, paint a detailed picture of how to successfully implement AI to drive social impact.

Realizing AI's full potential in nonprofits requires more than technical know-how. It necessitates a deep understanding of these organizations' unique challenges and opportunities and a steadfast commitment to developing and deploying AI technologies ethically, responsibly, and sustainably. Navigating this complex landscape demands a strategic, human-centered approach that prioritizes the needs and values of the communities served.

Reflection on Advanced AI in the Nonprofit Sector

Craig Newmark, philanthropist and founder of Craig Newmark Philanthropies and craigslist, offers a thought-provoking perspective: "The future of good customer service might start with training large language models in what's available already. Then the next step would be committing experienced customer service reps to both helping with customer service and then

The symbiotic world of AI and nonprofits as imagined by prompts and DALL-E-3 generative AI.

training the language models in anything new that they've just learned, or maybe they're just clarifying what's already there."

This insight encapsulates the idea of AI as an enhancer and augmenter of human capabilities rather than a replacement. By strategically leveraging advanced AI technologies, nonprofits can streamline operations, improve service delivery, and amplify their social impact.

However, it is crucial to approach AI adoption with a clear understanding of its limitations and potential risks. Nonprofits must carefully consider issues such as prioritizing data privacy and security, algorithmic bias, and the ethical implications of AI-driven decision-making. Establishing robust governance frameworks, investing in AI literacy, and building a culture of responsible innovation are essential steps in ensuring that AI is deployed in a way that aligns with organizational values and serves the greater good.

Future Thought for AI and Nonprofits – Future Perspectives, Tips, and Inspiration for Social Impact

As we look to the future, AI advancements and the emergence of next-generation technologies will undoubtedly reshape the nonprofit landscape. AI's potential applications are vast and far-reaching, from enhancing efficiency and enabling data-driven decision-making to personalizing stakeholder engagement and revolutionizing service delivery.

AI has also already been incorporated into many programs and objects, creating new ways for organizations to operate. Drone technology, powered by AI, can revolutionize the delivery of aid and resources to remote or disaster-stricken areas, greatly improving the efficiency and effectiveness of relief efforts. AI can also be harnessed using vision and sound to monitor and protect wildlife, enabling nonprofits to understand better and respond to the needs of the species they aim to conserve. By integrating AI into their operational frameworks, nonprofits can optimize their resources, streamline processes, and maximize their impact.

KEY AREAS AI CAN DRIVE TANGIBLE IMPACT

Social Services and Healthcare: AI-powered tools can help nonprofits better understand and predict the needs of their communities, enabling more targeted and effective interventions. Machine learning algorithms' strengths in analyzing vast amounts of data to identify patterns and risk factors allow nonprofits to proactively address issues like homelessness, food insecurity, and mental health challenges. A data-driven approach can lead to more efficient resource allocation and improved beneficiary outcomes.

Messaging and Communication: The increasing use of AI for messaging and communication presents a significant opportunity for nonprofits. AI-powered chatbots and virtual assistants can provide support and information to stakeholders 24/7, improving engagement and accessibility. These tools can also personalize content and tailor messages based on individual preferences and behaviors, ultimately driving greater impact and fostering deeper connections with supporters. Personalizing communications can lead to increased donor engagement and satisfaction.

Donor Interactions: Emerging AI technologies will also facilitate end-user and donor interactions. AI-powered recommendation engines can help nonprofits suggest relevant content, events, and give opportunities to their supporters based on their interests and past engagement. This enhances the user experience and increases the likelihood of continued support and advocacy. By leveraging AI to deliver personalized and seamless experiences, nonprofits can cultivate long-term relationships with their stakeholders and inspire greater commitment to their cause.

Operational Efficiency: Nonprofit organizations can overcome some of the constraints of scarce resources, such as limited time, funding, and human capital by using AI. AI-driven automation streamlines repetitive and time-consuming tasks, freeing up staff to focus on higher-value activities. Additionally, AI's ability to process and analyze massive amounts of data enables nonprofits to extract valuable insights that inform strategic decision-making. Through AI technologies, nonprofits can optimize the allocation and utilization of their resources, ensuring that every dollar, hour, and team member contributes to the maximum extent possible toward achieving the organization's mission.

Evolving Donor Landscape: With the rise of cryptocurrency and other digital payment methods, how donors contribute to nonprofits will also evolve in the coming years. AI can help nonprofits navigate this changing landscape by providing insights into donor behavior and preferences and automating and streamlining the giving process. Furthermore, younger donors, more likely to give larger amounts at once, can be more effectively engaged through AI-powered personalization and targeted outreach. By understanding these evolving trends, nonprofits can adapt their fundraising strategies and ensure long-term sustainability.

The Internet of Things (IoT): IoT presents another exciting frontier for AI in the nonprofit sector. By connecting various devices and sensors, nonprofits can collect real-time data on the impact of their programs and services, enabling them to make data-driven decisions and continuously improve their offerings. AI can be used to analyze this data and provide actionable insights, helping nonprofits optimize their resources and maximize their impact. By harnessing the power of IoT and AI, nonprofits can gain a more granular understanding of their communities and develop targeted interventions that address the root causes of social issues.

The Future Workforce: AI will undoubtedly shape the workforce of the future, both within the nonprofit sector and beyond. As Beth Kanter and Julie Maurer noted, the increasing adoption of AI will place a premium on uniquely human skills such as creativity, critical thinking, and interpersonal communication. Nonprofits that invest in developing these skills within their teams will be well-positioned to thrive in an AI-driven world, leveraging the power of these technologies while also nurturing the human qualities essential to driving social change. By embracing a continuous learning and development culture, nonprofits can ensure their workforce is equipped to navigate the evolving landscape.

THE FUTURE OF AI IN NONPROFITS

Looking ahead, AI's potential to revolutionize the nonprofit sector is boundless. AI technologies promise to enhance operational efficiency and open new avenues for engagement, impact measurement, and service delivery.

Key Areas Where Machine Learning and AI-Powered Tools Can Drive Significant Impact

1. **Enhanced Decision-Making Through Predictive Analytics**
   • Provide near-instant processing of vast amounts of valuable historical data, identifying patterns and trends that may not be immediately apparent to human analysts.
   • Forecast future outcomes, such as donor behavior, program success rates, and resource requirements, enabling proactive decision-making.
   • Optimize resource allocation strategies, ensuring that funds and efforts are directed toward initiatives most likely to yield the greatest impact.
   • Assist in scenario planning, allowing nonprofits to simulate various scenarios and assess the potential outcomes of different strategic choices, facilitating more informed decision-making processes.

2. **Personalized Donor Engagement**
   • Analyze donor data, including demographics, giving history, and engagement patterns, to create targeted and personalized communication strategies.
   • Identify the most effective channels, messaging, and timing for each donor, increasing the likelihood of successful fundraising campaigns.
   • Give instant, personalized responses to donor inquiries, enhancing the donor experience and fostering stronger relationships.
   • Find potential major donors and suggest tailored cultivation strategies, maximizing the impact of fundraising efforts.

3. Operational Efficiency

- Automate repetitive and time-consuming tasks like data entry, document processing, and report generation, allowing nonprofit staff to focus on higher-value activities.
- Streamline grant writing processes by analyzing past successful grant applications and providing suggestions for improvement, increasing the chances of securing funding.
- Facilitate and automate accounting processes, detect anomalies, and provide real-time financial insights, reducing the risk of errors and enabling better financial decision-making.
- Optimize staff and volunteer management through intelligent scheduling and task allocation systems to ensure that the right people are assigned to the right tasks at the right time, maximizing productivity and impact.

4. Impact Measurement

- Track and measure program effectiveness in real time by analyzing large volumes of data from various sources, such as surveys, social media, and IoT devices.
- Identify key performance indicators and predict the likelihood of achieving desired outcomes, allowing data-driven program adjustments.
- Present complex impact data in an easily understandable format using data visualization tools to communicate impact more effectively to stakeholders.
- Help anticipate future needs, develop strategies to address them, and maximize impact proactively.

5. Crisis Response and Management

- Synthesize and analyze data from multiple sources in real time, such as social media, news outlets, and satellite imagery, to predict and detect crises like natural disasters or disease outbreaks.

- Streamline resource allocation during crises, ensuring that aid and support are directed to the areas and individuals most in need.
- Provide affected individuals with instant, personalized support, and information, helping to reduce the burden on human respondents.
- Coordinate logistics and supply chain management during crises, optimizing the distribution of essential goods and services and minimizing waste and inefficiencies.

6. **Staff Training and Support**
   - Provide personalized, adaptive learning experiences for nonprofit staff with learning management systems, tailoring training content and pace to individual needs and preferences.
   - Capture and share institutional knowledge through knowledge management systems, ensuring valuable expertise is retained and accessible to all staff members.
   - Create immersive training experiences using virtual reality (VR) and augmented reality (AR) technologies, allowing staff to practice and develop skills in realistic, low-risk environments.
   - Analyze staff performance data and give targeted feedback and recommendations for improvement, supporting continuous professional development.

7. **Community and Stakeholder Engagement**
   - Monitor online platforms like social media to gauge public opinion and sentiment toward a cause to inform communication and engagement strategies.
   - Learn from community feedback and suggestions, identify common themes and priorities, and enable nonprofits to tailor their programs and services to better meet community needs.
   - Facilitate online discussions and forums, fostering a sense of community and enabling stakeholders to collaborate and share ideas more effectively.

- Identify and engage with potential partners, supporters, and influencers, leveraging their networks and expertise to amplify impact.

8. Protecting and Preserving the Environment

- Monitor environmental conditions in real time, providing early warning of potential threats such as forest fires, oil spills, or pollution incidents.
- Examine satellite images and other remote sensing data to track changes in land use, deforestation rates, and wildlife populations, informing conservation strategies.
- Predict poaching activities by analyzing patterns in poacher behavior and using drones with vision or heat sensing to identify high-risk areas, enabling rangers to take proactive measures to protect endangered species.
- Model the potential impacts of climate change and other environmental factors through simulations, developing more effective mitigation and adaptation strategies.

9. Healthcare and Social Services

- Analyze large volumes of health data to identify trends and risk factors, enabling targeted interventions and programs for at-risk populations.
- Catch and contain problems and protect public health by proactively discovering and monitoring disease outbreaks and the spread of infectious diseases.
- Provide remote healthcare services to underserved communities via telemedicine platforms, increasing access to medical expertise and support.
- Identify individuals at risk of mental health issues or substance abuse through analyzing online and social media data, enabling timely support and resources.

While AI enables these and other powerful opportunities, it is critical to use these technologies with a clear understanding of their potential benefits and risks. Nonprofits should keep ethical considerations, such as data privacy, transparency, and algorithmic bias, top of mind to ensure that AI is used responsibly and equitably.

By collaborating with AI experts, policymakers, and other stakeholders, nonprofits can help shape the development and deployment of AI technologies in ways that align with their missions and values, ultimately amplifying their impact and driving positive social change.

The Role of Nonprofits in Shaping AI Policy and Practice

ADVOCACY AND POLICY CHANGE

AI can analyze public opinion and legislative activities to help nonprofits craft more effective advocacy strategies that resonate with policymakers and the public. As the nonprofit sector increasingly adopts AI technologies, organizations have an opportunity to shape AI policy and practice actively. Nonprofits are uniquely positioned to promote responsible AI development and deployment, particularly in privacy and data protection.

COLLABORATION WITH POLICYMAKERS TO SHAPE THE FUTURE OF THE SECTOR

Nonprofits can collaborate with policymakers and industry partners to establish clear guidelines for AI development.

ACTIVE ADVOCACY AND POLICY ENGAGEMENT

Actively engage in policy discussions and advocate for regulations that prioritize ethical AI development, including participating in public consultations, submitting policy recommendations, and building relationships with policymakers to raise awareness about AI's unique challenges and opportunities for the social sector.

BUILDING MULTI-STAKEHOLDER COALITIONS
Convene and participate in coalitions that bring together policymakers, industry leaders, AI researchers, and civil society organizations to serve as platforms for sharing knowledge, developing best practices, and advocating for responsible AI policies that address the needs of vulnerable communities.

DEVELOPING ETHICAL FRAMEWORKS AND GUIDELINES
Leverage social impact and ethical considerations expertise to develop practical frameworks and guidelines for responsible AI development that can provide concrete guidance to industry partners on data privacy, algorithmic bias mitigation, transparency, and accountability in AI systems.

PILOTING AND SHOWCASING RESPONSIBLE AI PRACTICES
Serve as test beds for piloting and showcasing responsible AI practices and implementing ethical AI solutions, demonstrating their positive impact and providing valuable case studies and evidence-based insights to inform policy discussions and industry standards.

PROMOTING AI LITERACY AND EDUCATION
Be valuable in educating policymakers and industry partners about AI's societal implications by organizing workshops, training sessions, and awareness campaigns to enhance their understanding of potential risks and ethical considerations and promote best practices for responsible AI development.

FACILITATING OPEN DIALOGUE AND COLLABORATION
Act as neutral conveners to facilitate open dialogue and collaboration between policymakers and industry partners, creating spaces for constructive discussions, fostering mutual understanding, and bridging the gap between technical expertise and social impact considerations.

Many nonprofits are already dedicated to protecting stakeholder privacy and responsibly using data. Their experience can guide the development of AI policies and best practices that prioritize privacy, security, and ethical data management. By advocating for strong privacy protections and leading by example, nonprofits can help ensure AI technologies respect individual rights and build trust.

Nonprofits can also promote transparency and accountability in AI systems by collaborating with industry partners and policymakers to establish clear guidelines and create mechanisms for ongoing monitoring and evaluation. This proactive approach ensures AI technologies align with their missions and values, benefiting the communities they serve.

Additionally, nonprofits can contribute to responsible AI development by investing in AI literacy and training for staff and establishing clear ethical guidelines for AI use within their organizations. With a thoughtful approach to AI, nonprofits can maximize its benefits and serve as a model for other sectors.

ESTABLISHING GUIDELINES

Establishing guidelines is a crucial first step, but ensuring their effective implementation and enforcement requires a multifaceted approach:

1. **Promote Transparency and Accountability**
   - **Publicly Available Guidelines:** Make the AI guidelines accessible to the public, stakeholders, and partners. This will foster transparency and allow for broader scrutiny and feedback.
   - **Impact Assessments:** Regularly assess AI systems to evaluate their adherence to the established guidelines. Publish the results of these assessments to demonstrate accountability and identify areas for improvement.
   - **Independent Audits:** Engage independent third-party auditors to review AI systems and practices for compliance with the guidelines. This provides an unbiased evaluation and strengthens accountability.

2. **Build Capacity and Foster a Culture of Ethical AI**
   - **Training and Education:** Invest in training programs for staff, volunteers, and partners on the ethical implications of AI and the importance of adhering to the guidelines.
   - **Ethical Review Boards:** Establish internal review boards or committees tasked with reviewing AI projects and ensuring they align with the ethical guidelines.
   - **Whistleblower Mechanisms:** Create safe and confidential channels for individuals to report potential violations of the AI guidelines without fear of reprisal.

3. **Collaboration and Enforcement Mechanisms**
   - **Industry Partnerships:** Work with technology providers and AI developers to integrate the guidelines into product development and deployment processes.
   - **Certification Programs:** Explore the development of certification programs that recognize organizations adhering to the established AI guidelines.
   - **Legal and Regulatory Frameworks:** Advocate for legislation and regulations that incorporate the ethical principles outlined in the guidelines and provide a legal basis for enforcement.

4. **Continuous Monitoring and Improvement:**
   - **Feedback Mechanisms:** Establish mechanisms for gathering feedback from stakeholders, including beneficiaries, staff, and the wider community, on the impact and effectiveness of the AI guidelines.
   - **Regular Reviews and Updates:** The AI guidelines should be reviewed and updated periodically to reflect evolving technological advancements, societal values, and best practices.
   - **Adaptive Governance:** Implement adaptive governance structures that allow flexibility and responsiveness to emerging challenges and opportunities in AI ethics.

By adopting these strategies, nonprofits can move beyond simply setting guidelines to creating a culture of responsible AI, ensuring that these powerful technologies are used to advance their missions and serve the greater good.

Ultimately, nonprofits' role in shaping AI policy and practice is critical to ensuring that these technologies are developed and deployed in ways that promote the public good. By bringing their unique perspectives, values, and expertise to the table, nonprofits can help guide the future direction of AI in a way that benefits all of society while staying true to their missions and the communities they serve.

In conclusion, the emergence of AI presents challenges and opportunities for the nonprofit sector. Like the relationship between hummingbirds and butterflies, the synergy between AI and nonprofits can lead to remarkable outcomes. By embracing these technologies and committing to their responsible development and deployment, nonprofits can unlock new efficiency, effectiveness, and impact levels. This harmonious integration can help organizations plant the seeds of innovation, nurture the growth of their initiatives, and ultimately bear the fruit of amplified social impact, much like how hummingbirds and butterflies symbiotically help ecosystems thrive by pollinating plants and fostering new growth.

We hope this book has provided a valuable resource and roadmap for nonprofit leaders, technology professionals, and anyone interested in harnessing the power of AI for social good. Drawing inspiration from the delicate dance between hummingbirds and butterflies, we can envision a future where those in the nonprofit ecosystem co-create with AI to accelerate progress toward achieving missions and improving the lives of countless individuals and communities worldwide.

Acknowledgments

Writing this book has been an incredible and inspiring adventure filled with discovery, learning, and collaboration. A huge thank you to everyone who shared their insights and expertise to make this possible.

To all the amazing nonprofit leaders, volunteers, supporters, board members, and donors working tirelessly to make things better globally – your passion and dedication are truly inspiring. This book is dedicated to you and the world-changing work you do every day. I hope these strategies and ideas help you harness AI to amplify your impact and achieve your missions more effortlessly.

Special thanks to the brilliant minds who shared their knowledge for this book: Allison Fine, Beth Kanter, Cal Al-Dhubaib, Caleb Gardner, Craig Newmark, Cyrus Kazi, Devin Thorpe, Jace Martin, Julie Maurer, Leon Wilson, Lotay Yang, Melanie McGee, Oxana Vusova, Patrick Callihan, Rock Christopher, Sean Gardner, Jason Feig, and Tondi Allen. Your collective wisdom has enriched this book, and it's an honor to feature your voices.

A heartfelt thank you to the dedicated team at Wiley for their hard work in bringing this book to life. Your guidance and feedback have been invaluable throughout this journey.

To my family and friends, thank you for your unwavering support and encouragement. Your loving-kindness kept me grounded and focused, even during those long stretches of AI research.

And to you, the reader – thank you for believing in the power of technology to create positive change. By picking up this book, you're showing your commitment to using AI for social good. Together, through innovation, ethics, and inclusion, we can build a future where every nonprofit can thrive and make an even greater impact. Let's get started!

With immense gratitude,
Amy Neumann

About the Author

Amy Neumann is an entrepreneur, keynote speaker, author, artist, and technology strategist with three decades of experience. She inspires World Changers to leverage innovation and engagement for faster, easier, and more inclusive mission work. Founder of Resourceful Nonprofit and Technology Inclusion, Amy helps nonprofits achieve their goals efficiently. As CEO of Good Plus Tech, she focuses on groundbreaking technologies, including AI, to solve global social impact challenges. Amy frequently speaks at conferences and has been quoted or featured in numerous publications, including *Harvard Business Review*. Her previous book, *Simple Acts to Change the World*, celebrates ideas for social good and equity.

Appendix

AI Resources for Nonprofits

AI Applications for Social Impact
- Benetech: benetech.org
- Charity: Water: charitywater.org
- Crisis Text Line: crisistextline.org
- DoSomething.org: dosomething.org
- Khan Academy: khanacademy.org
- Polaris Project: polarisproject.org
- Rainforest Connection: rfcx.org
- Thorn: thorn.org
- UNICEF Innovation Fund: unicefinnovationfund.org
- Wadhwani AI: wadhwaniai.org
- Wild Me: wildme.org
- World Food Programme: wfp.org

AI for Good Initiatives
- AI for Good Global Summit: aiforgood.itu.int
- Data.org: data.org
- DataKind: datakind.org
- Google AI for Social Good: https://ai.google/responsibility/social-good/
- IBM Watson for Social Good: https://ibm.com/watson/social-impact
- Microsoft AI for Good: https://microsoft.com/en-us/ai/ai-for-good
- Omdena: omdena.com
- Salesforce.org: salesforce.org

AI Learning Resources

◆ AI for Everyone (Coursera): https://coursera.com/learn/ai-for-everyone
◆ AI4K12: ai4k12.org
◆ Deep Learning AI: deeplearning.ai
◆ Elements of AI: elementsofai.com
◆ Fast.ai: fast.ai
◆ Kaggle Learn: https://kaggle.com/learn
◆ Khan Academy: khanacademy.org
◆ MIT OpenCourseware: https://ocw.mit.edu/index.htm
◆ Microsoft AI School: aischool.microsoft.com
◆ Stanford Online: online.stanford.edu

AI News and Media

◆ AI in Business: https://emerj.com/artificial-intelligence-podcast/
◆ AI Magazine: https://aaai.org/ojs/index.php/aimagazine
◆ Future Today Institute: https://futuretodayinstitute.com/trends
◆ Inside AI: https://inside.com/ai
◆ Lex Fridman Podcast: https://lexfridman.com/podcast
◆ MIT Technology Review: https://technologyreview.com/topic/artificial-intelligence/
◆ Synced: syncedreview.com
◆ The AI Alignment Podcast: ai-alignment.com
◆ The Batch (Deeplearning.ai): https://deeplearning.ai/the-batch
◆ The TWIML AI Podcast: twimlai.com
◆ VentureBeat: https://venturebeat.com/category/ai

AI Research Institutions

◆ Allen Institute for AI: allenai.org
◆ DeepMind: deepmind.com
◆ Facebook AI Research (FAIR): https://ai.facebook.com/research

- MIT Media Lab: media.mit.edu
- Mila - Quebec Artificial Intelligence Institute: https:// mila.quebec/en/
- OpenAI: openai.com
- Stanford AI Lab: ai.stanford.edu

AI Tools and Platforms

- Amazon Web Services (AWS) for Nonprofits: https://aws .amazon.com/government-education/nonprofits/ nonprofit-credit-program/
- Google for Nonprofits: https://google.com/nonprofits
- Meta for Nonprofits: https://facebook.com/government-nonprofits/best-practices/nonprofits
- Microsoft Azure AI for Nonprofits: https://microsoft.com/ en-us/nonprofits/azure
- GPT Playground: https://openai.com/api
- Poe: poe.com

Blogs and Podcasts

- AI in Business: https://emerj.com /artificial-intelligence-podcast/
- Beth Kanter's Blog: https://bethkanter.org/blog/category/ ai-beginner/
- Lex Fridman Podcast: https://lexfridman.com/podcast
- Stanford Social Innovation Review (SSIR): https://ssir .org/topics/entry/artificial_intelligence
- The AI Alignment Podcast: ai-alignment.com
- The TWIML AI Podcast: twimlai.com

Community and Events

- AI Ethics Global Conference: aiethicsglobal.com
- AI for Good Community: https://aiforgood.itu.int/community
- Data Science for Social Good: dssg.uchicago.edu
- RE•WORK Summits: https://re-work.co/events
- The Good AI: goodai.com

Educational Resources and Courses

- Coursera: coursera.org
- edX: edx.org
- Fast.ai: fast.ai
- LinkedIn: https://linkedin.com/learning/topics/artificial-intelligence
- Khan Academy: https://khanacademy.org
- Udacity: udacity.com

Funding and Support

- Chan Zuckerberg Initiative: chanzuckerberg.com
- MacArthur Foundation: macfound.org
- Omidyar Network: omidyar.com
- Patrick J. McGovern Foundation: mcgovern.org
- Schmidt Futures: schmidtfutures.com
- Skoll Foundation: skoll.org

International Perspectives

- AI for All (Global): ai-for-all.org
- CIFAR (Canada): cifar.ca
- European AI Alliance: https://digital-strategy.ec.europa.eu/en/policies/european-ai-alliance
- Max Planck Institute for Intelligent Systems (Germany): https://is.mpg.de/en
- The Alan Turing Institute (UK): turing.ac.uk

News and General Information

- Harvard Business Review: https://hbr.org/topic/subject/technology-and-analytics
- MIT Technology Review: https://technologyreview.com/topic/artificial-intelligence
- Stanford Social Innovation Review (SSIR): https://ssir.org/topics/entry/artificial_intelligence
- The Brookings Institution: https://brookings.edu/research/artificial-intelligence
- Wired: https://wired.com/category/artificial-intelligence

Nonprofit-Specific Resources

- Microsoft Skills Hub: https://microsoft.com/nonprofits
- NetHope: nethope.org
- NTEN: nten.org
- TechSoup: techsoup.org

Index